WHEN YOU PUT ON A RED SHIRT

Keith Dewhurst

When You Put on a Red Shirt

The Dreamers and their Dreams:
Memories of Matt Busby,
Jimmy Murphy and
Manchester United

YELLOW JERSEY PRESS
LONDON

Published by Yellow Jersey Press 2009

2 4 6 8 10 9 7 5 3 1

Copyright © Keith Dewhurst 2009

Keith Dewhurst has asserted his right under the Copyright,
Designs and Patents Act 1988 to be identified as the author of this work

First published in Great Britain in 2009 by
Yellow Jersey Press
Random House, 20 Vauxhall Bridge Road,
London SW1V 2SA

www.rbooks.co.uk

Addresses for companies within The Random House Group
Limited can be found at:
www.randomhouse.co.uk/offices.htm

The Random House Group Limited Reg. No. 954009

A CIP catalogue record for this book
is available from the British Library

ISBN 9780224082839

The Random House Group Limited supports The Forest Stewardship
Council (FSC), the leading international forest certification organisation.
All our titles that are printed on Greenpeace approved FSC certified paper
carry the FSC logo. Our paper procurement policy can be found at
www.rbooks.co.uk/environment

Mixed Sources
Product group from well-managed
forests and other controlled sources
www.fsc.org Cert no. TT-COC-2139
© 1996 Forest Stewardship Council
FSC

Typeset in Bembo by Palimpsest Book Production Limited,
Grangemouth, Stirlingshire
Printed and bound in Great Britain by
Clays Ltd, St Ives plc

Contents

Prologue: In the United Museum

If David Lloyd George was the most charismatic person I ever laid eyes on, his Merlin-like magic obvious even to a five-year-old, Matt Busby was the most charismatic I have known, when he was the manager of Manchester United and I was a reporter travelling with the team. Yet he was never my hero, because I knew how ruthless he had been in the creation of his myth and power base. My hero was his assistant Jimmy Murphy, who had charge of the team after the Munich air crash, when I sat up at night with him in the hotels, and he would talk about football, dreams and Matt's ambiguous nature; and to sustain our sorrow and puzzlement he would order whisky and sugar and hot water.

Half a lifetime later, on a damply cold February evening, I made my way to Old Trafford and a ceremony that would honour Jimmy's memory. I had written for the old *Manchester Evening Chronicle*, and my colleague on the *Evening News* had been David Meek, who stayed with the job until his retirement. Thanks to him I had an invitation to the unveiling in the United museum of Jimmy's portrait bust.

I went on the tram and walked up past the deserted cricket ground and the former Stretford Town Hall, where the neon faces of the clock tower each showed a different time. Across the railway bridge is a branch of the United Megastore, which stands where in 1966 Jimmy leaned on the railings and explained to me before anyone thought it possible why England would win the World Cup. Further on, at the old scoreboard end, spotlights enhanced the larger-than-life statue of Busby, with its extraordinary sexual swagger of the hips, which I suppose is a pretty shrewd comment, and above it the huge red neon said MANCHESTER UNITED. I realised again the crushing size of the stadium. Because it was never planned in one go its accretions express corporate expansion and success. Shuttered but illuminated it is like a military compound. It over-reaches the railway concourse, the cobbled back road, the site of a former factory. It has consumed them. They no longer exist.

At the museum entrance the security staff were affable enough, but what they would have been like if I had not had my letter of invitation I do not know. Upstairs, at the turnstiles, there were warmer smiles but a check-list of names. I was waved on. The decor was curved and plastic, the flooring heavy-duty industrial, the lights hidden. There was football action on big screens, and sounds everywhere: the roar of the crowd or triumphal music. It was like being inside a computer game, or maybe one of those CIA thrillers in which one isn't sure who is the goody and who the baddy. There was nowhere to hang a coat. Everyone else had come in cars and not worn one, I supposed.

Not that I recognised a soul, or that anyone looked at me twice. They were strangers in suits and they exhibited a familiar provincial blend of cheeriness and embarrassment. A beaten-looking man in a leather jacket and no tie seemed as uncertain as I was. Others were confident, because for them the evening was a justification, a rare invitation to be on the inside again. One of them, ravaged and leaning on a stick, pressed a computer screen to download his own biography. I saw that he was the goalkeeper I had watched in the youth team even before I joined the newspaper.

Then a warm smiling middle-aged woman hurried across to me and held my hand. It was Pat, Jimmy Murphy's eldest daughter, and I laughed with pleasure.

'Steve Richards is here,' she said. 'He was the dark good-looking one and you were the fair good-looking one.'

Meaning reporters.

'What's the bust like?' I said.

It was commissioned after a campaign by the Former Players' Association to have Jimmy honoured. They had wanted his name on the rebuilt North Stand. The board had refused but agreed to a bust. Since Jimmy had been dead for a while, the sculptor must have done it from photographs.

'Well, it's very good from the side,' said Pat, 'but we're not so sure about the front.'

Actually, I thought, it would have taken Rodin himself to capture that choler and portly dignity, those flashes of inspiring charm; and to make the metal seem about to emit the trademark throaty chuckle.

'There's not a day goes by,' I said, 'that I don't think about him.'

'I know,' she said. 'I know you must.'

I asked her about the man in the leather jacket. She told me who it was: someone whose youth games I had reported, and who failed after a few moments of glory in the first team. He really had been a good-looker, I always thought, but now he seemed plain and deadened.

At the actual unveiling I stood between two men who looked familiar and I realised that one was Alex Ferguson and the other Pat Crerand. Martin Edwards bade us a deft, corporate welcome, and one of Jimmy's sons made a splendid speech in which he said that the bust was a tribute not to his father but to an entire back-room staff. He named them, the dead and the retired, and he called them the Manchester United family. Then Pat and her sister pulled the cords to reveal the bust.

'See that?' said Pat Crerand.

'What?' said Ferguson.

'That's you in thirty years.'

'Och away with you,' said Ferguson.

After that reunions came thick and fast. The retired laundry ladies introduced themselves by their nicknames. 'Hello, Keith. It's Omo and Daz!' Mrs Burgess, tea lady, cleaner and factotum, said, 'Do you remember? Jimmy used to say, "Keith's here, better make that cup a pot."' Wilf McGuinness, who literally lost his hair after Matt had him sacked as manager, talked about the afternoon of the Munich disaster, when he sat and wept in our newspaper office. Wilf is massively outgoing, and as a summariser on United Radio he used to deliver judgements such as 'This defence is like Dracula: it's afraid of crosses.' Bobby Charlton, whose articles I used to ghost, wore a grey bespoke suit and said I didn't look any older (liar), and Shay Brennan waved his big cigar. Nobby Stiles was about to go to Dubai to make an after-dinner speech. A small shock-haired man turned out to be the son of Joe Armstrong, the legendary back-room man and Jimmy Murphy's fixer. Johnny

Doherty, at that time very active in the Former Players' Association and one of the first Busby Babes, told me that he made his debut for United against a Middlesbrough team that included George Hardwick, Wilf Mannion and the goalkeeper Umberto Ugolini, this last name rolled ripely around a classic northern tongue. United were captained by Johnny Carey and after the match Doherty went home on the bus. 'Not,' he said pointedly, 'a Ferrari.' As we talked Les Olive came by. He took over as club secretary after Munich, and eventually went on the board. He said, 'Are you still writing?'

'Of course.'

'Match reports?' said Les.

'Films,' snarled Johnny on my behalf.

Les slid on with an alarmed grin.

'None of Denis Law's own souvenirs in here,' said Johnny. 'Had you noticed?'

This was because the Former Players did not get money from the museum, of course; and the political frisson between the board and the Association had a serious as well as a comedy-show side. Johnny's sidekick on the Association was the delightful David Sadler. He was signed as a centre forward and turned into a defender. Jimmy gave him one of the classic pieces of advice.

'David,' he said, 'they can't score when the ball's in the stand.'

And of course I talked long with Billy Foulkes, my old pal – in Jimmy's phrase, my closest among the players – who survived the Munich crash and on the long journeys after made up a card school with me and David Meek and Jack Crompton the trainer.

'There's a lot of falling-over nowadays,' said Bill, 'but nobody gets kicked. Not really.'

You should know, I thought, remembering how he clattered his man at the San Siro in 1958, whereupon the crowd threw vegetables over the wire.

More than thirty members of the Murphy clan went to the unveiling, with their cameras and their sense of justice having been done. I was told that in his last years Jimmy had lured one of his daughters-in-law into whisky, sugar and hot water, and there were glimpses of him in all his sons, above all of his warmth.

Next day the newspapers announced that United had become by annual turnover the world's richest football club, and in the years since then Mrs Burgess went to Monte Carlo to receive a UEFA Long Service Medal, Shay Brennan, Les Olive and Johnny Doherty have died, the money in football has got bigger, and there has been the drama of the Glazer takeover.

In March 2007 I saw United beat Roma 7–1 with glittering football that showed another great side in the making. From my seat I talked on a mobile to David Meek, high above me on press-box hospitality duty. I asked him about one of our old chums I'd last met at the unveiling, and he said, 'I'm afraid he's beginning to forget things.' I had to blink back a tear, but all through the game I thought how good it was that David and I have kept our friendship, and how lucky we were, when we were young, to have been touched by something mysterious: a genuine modern version of the ancient myths: the life, death and perpetual rebirth of heroes.

PART ONE
Before Munich

The press conference

I first heard the name Matt Busby the day after United announced his appointment as manager. It was 1945 and I was in our classroom at Oakwood Park, to which my second-class boarding school had been evacuated. It was a grey day and rain swept down the valley and gave the landward mass of Conway Mountain a sodden peaty colour. In the mid-morning break desks banged and my friend Peter and his older, clumsier brother David rushed up with a newspaper. They said that United, which they had just begun to support, had signed this wonderful person to manage them and would now be very successful, so I should make up my mind and be a fan.

I don't know what newspaper it was, probably the *News Chronicle* or the *Daily Dispatch*, and I'm not sure why Peter and David had decided to support United. Perhaps it was because United would be in the First Division when proper football restarted, and Manchester City in the Second, or perhaps it was because Peter and David lived in the affluent suburb of Hale, and their stepfather had a nodding acquaintance with James Gibson, the businessman who had come to United's rescue in the 1930s.

I am sure that what they read out from the paper was

Busby's statement at his first press conference, when he said that he would make the club great again by developing his own young players.

It was a fabulous moment, of course: Odysseus declaiming his own odyssey, the football equivalent of Napoleon's Proclamation to the Army of Italy, the deliberate beginning of a myth, a first, brilliant pre-emptive strike at rewriting history. Not denying history exactly, never explicitly denying it, but knowing that his personality would capture the journalists and sweep them along; playing on the provincial arrogance that they were the best judges, drawing them into the remembrance of what some of them had seen and even played against, the attacking football of the United team that had won the Cup in 1909, and the way football had been before the slump of the 30s, when the stopper centre half and niggardly defensive play ruined the spectacle and denied the emotions their release. To all this, Matt seemed to say, and to the domination of metropolitan Arsenal, I will put an end, and you will be my apostles and spread the word.

The Manchester to which he spoke had changed little since the end of the First World War, and was to seem the same for another decade and more. It preserved the landscape and the habits of the world's first shocking industrial civilisation, and it was dying, dead, even though we were still its living people. We were the last creations of Cottonopolis. We had seen cotton waste blowing in the street and heard the din of machinery driven by steam engines.

Matt ignited the final flame of that historic city's greatness, and he could do so because Manchester was still a thriving press centre, with two evening papers, its own dailies and Sundays and its printings of all the nationals. Its football writers included Ivan Sharpe, who at Derby County had played with John Goodall and Steve Bloomer, two of early football's superstars, a man of high knowledge like Archie Ledbrooke, the brilliant showman journalist Henry Rose, originals like George Follows and Eric Thompson, who illustrated his reports with cartoons, and in H. D. Davies, "Old International" of the *Manchester Guardian*, an actual literary stylist. Some of these men had been in football for longer than Matt himself. They did not mess about with off-the-field muckraking, and although some of their prose was purple, there was a genuine culture of opinion and match reports rooted in experience.

The players were on fixed wages with no freedom of contract. A few very famous ones did ghosted articles and appeared in adverts, but chequebook journalism was minimal, and agents using reporters to start destabilising rumours was a horror of the future. Once I was sent by our newsroom to interview Don Revie about a story that he was seeking a transfer from Manchester City. He would not speak to me because I was not empowered to offer him money. The news editor did not blame me. He took the view that even if Revie was going (he did) the exclusive wasn't worth the asking price. On the other hand, Revie may have been notorious even then.

Football itself may have festered with illegal payments but the papers were surprisingly innocent. We were in a different culture, and a different mode of time and distance. In 1950 it took as long to get to London as it does to reach New York today. We did not read the London newspapers. We saw few reports of matches between southern teams. There were live radio commentaries but no television. Cinema newsreels showed the goals and near misses in cup finals and internationals but that was it. What was happening in Milan (i.e., the future of football) might as well have been on another planet, and uncles or cousins or friends at work who had actually seen great players or great matches were sought out and their memories talked over many times.

In this context we can understand both the slow take-up and the originality of Busby's spin-doctoring. In the 1930s Herbert Chapman, the great manager of Arsenal, had publicised his team with one imaginative stroke after another, such as getting the local Underground station called Arsenal, but Matt was more subtle. The public knew about Arsenal, but felt a part of United, a conviction which deepened with the years and explains the hostility to the Glazers. People say Matt Busby suspected journalists, but that is too simple a view, and in my opinion his affection for that great generation of Manchester sports writers was as real as his sorrow when most of them died at Munich. His handling of them was nonetheless brilliant.

Take Henry Rose of the *Daily Express*, a flamboyant personality whose excesses seemed stunts but were in fact prophetic of sports journalism to come, a good example being his treatment of the United centre forward Tommy Taylor. Taylor had a long spell of poor form, and only recovered his touch in the weeks before Munich; but, as Jimmy told me, Matt refused to drop him because of his influence on the other players. During his poor run Taylor scored three times for England against Denmark, and Rose's opinion appeared under the headline DROP HAT-TRICK TAYLOR.

Jimmy told me how angry Busby had been at this, but how he hid his feelings, joshed Rose along, and made him privy to his reasons for keeping the player in the team. That was the spin and the charm turned upon one person; the entire operation was of course more profound. It was both far-sighted and off the cuff somehow, because if Matt was the man for the hour, United's history and situation gave him everything he needed.

Ancient history

In the first place there was lost but still remembered glory. United had been formed from the old railway employees' club Newton Heath by a shrewd, straw-hatted, cigar-chewing manager named Ernest Mangnall and his backer J. H. Davies, a brewery magnate. The ground was in Bank Street, Clayton, the site of today's National Cycling Centre. It was overlooked by a chemical works whose thirty chimneys spread steam and foul stenches on match days. The club lagged behind Manchester City until 1906, when fortunes changed. United were promoted to the First Division, and City were punished for a series of illegal payments and bribery scandals. They were made to auction the players involved, and Mangnall snapped up four of them, including the great right-winger Billy Meredith. Meredith and centre half Charlie Roberts were superstars, and there are potent photographs of them in that part of the museum where I chatted with Johnny Doherty. Around them Mangnall built a team that won the League twice and the Cup once, and played beautiful attacking football that people remembered all their lives. One of them was Vittorio Pozzo, an engineering student in Manchester, who in the 1930s became manager of Italy and won two World Cups.

United's success encouraged them to move in 1910 to Old Trafford, an enormous stadium designed by Archibald Leitch and described as the finest in the world. On the edge of a new industrial estate, it cost £60,000 and its facilities included a billiards room, a gymnasium, a massage room and a plunge bath. People in London, reported the *Manchester Guardian*, were sneering at 'moneybags United'. A year later Mangnall quarrelled with the directors and left, and the club began a long decline.

Memories of Mangnall's team, however, lived on. When I was a teenager old men talked about it, local newspapers often recalled it, and Billy Meredith, who played until he was almost fifty and did not die until months after the Munich crash, was a legend. When I was a reporter I heard gossip about him most weeks, because his son-in-law owned the tobacconist's opposite our office. Later, in the early 1960s, after I had left the paper, I had a curious personal link with Mangnall's team, because his left back Vince Hayes was our neighbour in Kersal, Salford. Over eighty, he had come to live with his daughter, and had a dipping walk from the broken leg that had ended his playing career. He kept his chin tilted, as though still surveying the forwards bearing down on him, and wore a trilby and an old mac, and carried shopping in a leather bag. As I walked at his pace he would tell me about his coaching days in Norway, Vienna and Madrid.

When football resumed after the Great War United's coffers were empty and the mortgage on the ground uncleared. They were relegated, but struggled back and by 1927 had halved the mortgage. Then J. H. Davies died and with him his guarantees. With Lancashire in economic decline United could not progress. In October 1930, the team having lost eleven successive games, the supporters' club called for a boycott. Attendances plummeted. On the last day of the season, in May 1931, less than 4,000 people were in Mangnall's mighty stadium, and the team were relegated.

Matt Busby watched these events from Manchester City, where he was a player, and twenty-odd years later he would talk about the boycott with genuine alarm. The very idea of it seemed to him to be a threat to good order, and was the reason he was opposed for so long to any kind of supporters' organisation.

United's crisis came on Friday, 18 December 1931, six days before I was born. The club owed some £30,000 and the secretary Walter Crickmer was turned away when he went to the bank for money to pay the wages. Over the ensuing weekend an approach was made to James Gibson, a businessman with clothing and engineering interests. He paid the wages and told the newspapers that if there was public support he would provide more. The Christmas Day fixture drew a big crowd and Gibson was committed. 'A football interest,' he said, 'is a very important factor in maintaining contented and healthy-minded working people.' If the club had found a patriarch, what the patriarch found were three out-of-the-ordinary football men.

Harold Hardman, a city-centre solicitor, was a board member. Before 1914 he had played as an amateur for

Everton and United, and won two England caps and an Olympic gold medal. He was spare, acerbic, pithy and principled, but never a natural politician. Years later, Busby's schemes to circumvent him led to the takeover of United by Louis Edwards, and everything that followed.

Louis Rocca, colourful and vulgar, came from Manchester's Little Italy and had been the office boy when United were still at Newton Heath. His official capacity was chief scout, but that was a cover-all title for a street-wise Catholic fixer: it was Rocca who at the end of 1944 wrote the guarded letter that apprised Matt Busby of the waiting managership.

Walter Crickmer, club secretary, who died at Munich aged 62, was a decent, ordinary-seeming man with a sense of the future, and of football as spectacle, more than just a working man's rush. A small example was the programme he masterminded for the 1939 Cup semi-final at Old Trafford. It was more lavish than the norm, more decorative, with more to read. He was also United's manager for a couple of spells, and he believed in the development of young players.

In fact, the earliest mention of a youth policy was made at James Gibson's first board meeting at the end of 1931. The notion was to run 'a colts or nursery team from next season . . . so that a common idea and technique shall unite the junior with the senior members of the playing staff'. The word 'colts' has a middle-class, boarding-school sort of ring to it, and was surely Gibson's.

Today a youth team seems an obvious necessity and expense, but eighty years ago that was not the general opinion. Big clubs relied on smaller teams and lower divisions to produce players. To develop their own seemed wasteful, given the failure rate. It is also a curious fact that although British coaches like Vince Hayes had worked abroad since before 1914, it took years for coaching as a profession to be accepted at home. We know how to play, ran the argument. We invented the game. We do not need to be taught. Professional football was provincial, working class and out of touch with the country's educated elites, who played rugger and cricket, don't you know. A great manager like Herbert Chapman found players young if he could, but most of his key men were bought ready-made and slotted into ingenious tactical formations. He was a deep and explicit thinker about the game, but most people were not, and coaching and player appraisal were random, as Busby knew from his own career.

Manchester City bought him as a teenage inside forward and for two years he was a complete failure. Then one day a player could not turn up for the third team, and Matt had to take his place at wing half, a position which at once revealed his considerable gifts. As a manager Matt turned several inside forwards into fullbacks, notably the great Johnny Carey himself, but compared to his methods the running of even a successful 1930s team like Manchester City was haphazard. No wonder Chapman's Arsenal ruled the roost.

Chapman had knowledge, authority, organisation, a flair for publicity and a sense of football as part of a wider entertainment industry. As a coach he created a defend and counter-attack system that his successors took into the 1950s. Not until Jimmy Murphy created a form of 'total football' twenty-odd years before the Dutch, did anyone find a tactical way past

Arsenal, and outside the metropolis it was hard to match them for glamour and financial power.

Concentration upon youth development was surely a reaction to Arsenal's might, and at the end of the 30s it brought success. Preston North End won the 1938 Cup Final with young Scotsmen including Bill Shankly, and the 1939 Final was contested by Portsmouth and Wolves, both of whom had many apprentices.

United, at the end of that season, finished fourteenth in the First Division. But the reserves had won the Central League for the first time in eighteen years, the A team had won the Manchester League, and the colts, the Manchester United Junior Athletic Club, had won the Chorlton League. At the annual general meeting James Gibson said, 'We have no intention of buying any more mediocrities. In years to come we will have a Manchester United composed of Manchester players.'

Then the war came. Regular football stopped. The MUJAC was disbanded, although Crickmer played what young talent he could muster in a factory team named Goslings. In December 1941 Old Trafford was bombed: there were craters in the pitch and the centre stand was destroyed. The club was run from temporary offices in a cold store owned by James Gibson, and the board met in the old rooms beneath the covered corner of the ground at the scoreboard end. Later, Walter Crickmer had an office built out onto the terraces, and a Nissen hut next to the railway served as a gym, in which Jimmy Murphy was to coach the team that won the Cup in 1948, marking a pitch on the floor and walking people through moves like the famous Delaney–Rowley switch. But for almost ten years matches had to be played at Manchester City's Maine Road. The old boardroom, as it was known when I went to Old Trafford every day, may well have been the former sneered-at billiards room, because it was like something in a Victorian hotel in the Lake District. Off it there was a curious cubbyhole: Jimmy Murphy's office, to which Mrs Burgess brought the pot of tea.

James Gibson's chairmanship was not like that of J. H. Davies, which had been an attempt to buy instant success. Gibson was idealistic, conservative and financially cautious: in his first years Busby made only one cheapish transfer foray, to buy the mercurial winger Jimmy Delaney, whom most people had unwisely written off. When he sold Johnny Morris for a record £25,000, one of the reasons was that the club would not pay under-the-counter bonuses.

Gibson died in 1951, to be succeeded by Harold Hardman, another stickler, and I do not think that the early Babes were assembled by very much in the way of bungs; it was as much a case of charm, dream-weaving and being in there first. After 1961, when players became free to negotiate their own wages, United were never among the highest payers. One might well say that the financial caution of the Martin Edwards and PLC regimes had its roots in the 1930s, and the Glazers, of course, have their own reasons to stick to a business plan.

Overall, when we recall this history, and consider that of the team that won the Cup in 1948 seven were Walter Crickmer youth players and three had been bought as teenagers pre-war, we might want to view Matt's famous first press conference in another light.

What he did was to state established club policy.

That he contrived to make this seem an invention and

the beginning of a crusade, the dream that still goes on, expresses both the magic and darkness of his persona, and is an index of his genius.

Teenager

To tell the truth, boarding-school boys did not count for much at the end of the war. There was no consumer youth culture, and I suppose that one reason that Peter and I came to support Manchester United is that it was something of our own that was unlike our immediate backgrounds. His stepfather was a rentier, my father and the men in my mother's family cotton-trade managers and salesmen. Their parents, born in the 1860s, had lifted themselves above the working mass. The educations they bought us were proof of success and they were hurt when it led us to question their values. They hated the Labour government and did not want us to have exploratory thoughts. We were brainy, but at our school hearty success at games still counted for more, and the game was rugby. We didn't know any girls and had few opportunities to meet them. We wanted to be different, and professional football fitted our bill.

In my case it took a while. Peter and David went to numerous matches but I was timid. I had further to travel home, a long bus ride in the cigarette fug of the top deck, through the sooty canyons of the business district, past the novelist Mrs Gaskell's house in the seediness of what had been in the 1840s an affluent suburb, along the main road where desert-camouflaged Afrika Korps prisoners had laid tramlines, and to Stockport and the open country beyond. Nor were my parents very keen. Deep down they were afraid of the crowd, the working mass that was supposed to threaten us. So was I, but in the autumn of 1946 I braved it. I was fourteen. We sat in expensive seats because David said it was safest. It rained and on a leaden pitch United beat Middlesbrough by the only goal, scored on the turn by Jack Rowley from a square pass by Johnny Hanlon.

At the end we left early to avoid the crush. I looked back from the top of the steps. Charlie Mitten's feet flickered as he held off two defenders, and shouting men towered round me. In that instant, because I did not understand why they were shouting, I determined to make myself a connoisseur and I realised that I was hooked.

I knew without being told that this was the art of the common people, a thing as varied in action, ideas, events and personalities as the epic poems of the past, except that the poems were fixed and written, and this was a passing show. Its heroes were mortal but heroes nonetheless, and there was an ideal. The thing could be done effectively but physically, or it could strive for perfection, for a skill and a beauty in motion that seemed to make time stand still and death await another day.

The great players, Jimmy Murphy reiterated in so many hotels and dingy offices, are the ones who play the game in their own time. Manchester United, one soon saw, were the team in England who strove most mightily for that heart-stopping perfection. They are the only club to have done it throughout the entire sixty years since

I first saw them. That, and not because they win things, is why they are hated, and why they are important for football as a whole.

When we were away at school we had the *Manchester Evening Chronicle* football pink delivered for us to collect on Sunday, and it was a ritual to go to an out-of-bounds milk bar called Adneys and read every page. Eric Todd was the travelling reporter with Manchester City, and Alf Clarke had been with United since their lowest days. We educated boys laughed at Alf's outrageous bias and at the old-style journalese: the number of times the rigging was shaken or Frank Swift jumped literally from nowhere. Another thing that made us laugh was a brief radio interview we heard about a pre-war match in which West Bromwich Albion scored six goals in the last five minutes. The man who had played in the match had a comically husky voice and an astounded intonation, and when he appeared in United's pre-season souvenir team photo he was in the back row in a collar and tie, and it said J. MURPHY (Coach).

During school holidays we went to as many games as we could afford, City as well as United, and to make our money go further we stopped sitting in the great Maine Road Stand and went on the popular side. We would arrive about two hours before kick-off to ensure that we stood above an entrance and had an un-interrupted view. From there we saw some famous victories, notably the demolition of Burnley on New Year's Day 1948, and the defeat of Chelsea the week before United won the Cup.

We had our first sight of Busby some time in 1947, when we were sitting at the front of the Maine Road

Stand and he was in the directors' box. The match was against Sheffield United, and our team played badly and were beaten. We were in a disappointed rage and Busby's calmness amazed us. Everything on the field went wrong but he puffed his pipe without any expression. What a gift it was, that ability to hide his feelings, and what a difference from today's gesticulators and screamers with advertising logos all over their clothes, although to be fair, George Kay, the manager under whom Busby played at Liverpool, is said to have shouted throughout every game.

That day so long ago Matt wore a light overcoat and a soft hat in those shades of brown that suited him so well. Before Munich he trained and played in five-a-sides in a tracksuit, but he always wore street clothes on match days, either a suit or a club blazer and flannels. He had an eye for an expensive pair of shoes, I came to notice, and at the height of his fame drove a Jensen Interceptor.

Jimmy Murphy, alas, or perhaps because of the comic value not alas, was a great shouter from the bench. Bill Foulkes told me at the bust unveiling that the first time he played for United Reserves he thought that there was trouble in the crowd until he realised that it was Jimmy coaching from the line. A classic instance of Jimmy's good intentions gone wrong occurred in a Cup tie after Munich, when he resolved to sit in the stand but then appeared at full trot in the tunnel, yelling to trainer Jack Crompton, 'Jack, Jack, they're getting strung out!' United's best on-field shouter during my time with them was, perhaps inevitably, Wilf McGuinness. I remember during one of those lulls into which any crowd will fall at one time or another Wilf's voice rang out typical and true:'Lads, cut out the fanny, lads!'

The fanny, over-elaboration or unnecessary shortness in passing, was indeed a heinous crime in Murphy's book. He liked a long-ball game, in a way, although he emphasised that to play it well was more difficult than to play short, because of the margin for error. He startled me once by observing that the long-ball game as practised by Wolverhampton Wanderers in the 1950s was more difficult to achieve than what the Brazilians did. This was after, as manager of Wales, he had met the Brazilians in the 1958 World Cup and used what he called a retreating defence against them. That was another game at which his voice echoed around a thinly populated stadium. 'Cliff!' he yelled, as the winger Cliff Jones ran with his head down. 'Cliff! What the fuck are you doing, Cliff?'

Ever since that conversation about the Brazilians I have studied them with care, and saw them in the 1998 World Cup Semi-Final in Marseilles, when the Dutch could have won, I thought, if they had attacked more in extra time. But they were wary of Brazil's reputation. That reputation became awesome after the World Cup Final of 1970. Yet to me this final has always posed the biggest mystery of football in my time: why did the Italians, the expert man-markers, stand off the Brazilian playmaker Gerson, and give him the freedom of the Aztec Stadium? Similarly, it has always seemed to me to be a pity that Pelé never played club football in Italy or Spain. Had he faced those defences week in and week out he might have proved himself the player of the twentieth century. As it is, I think that both di Stéfano and Maradona have better claims to the title.

★   ★   ★

United's 1948 season began well but fell into a slump, whereupon Busby made his second great statement to the press: to Alf Clarke, in fact, from whom the other papers carried it on. 'It is a loss of rhythm,' Busby said, 'and everything will soon come right.'

It did, with a series of shattering victories that culminated in the Cup Final. Two reputations were established: that of Busby for wisdom, and that of the team for its beautiful attacking football. Old-time journalists like Ivan Sharpe said that it was the best since 1914.

Then Morris was sold, Charlie Mitten did a runner to Bogotá to make money, Johnny Anderson, who had only come into the team for that one hard-hitting season, did not hold his form, and the miraculous underlying balance was gone. There were marvellous displays, better than the others could provide, but the League title was elusive. In April 1950 we saw crucial and dulling defeats at Old Trafford against Portsmouth and Birmingham City, and when United did take the Championship in 1952 it was with a surge that was obviously the last hurrah for players like Carey, Cockburn, Rowley and Stan Pearson.

Young man

In 1950 I went from school to Cambridge and a year later Peter joined me. Until 1953 we shared a set of rooms in Peterhouse, where my time both shaped me for ever and was wasted. I had won a college exhibition but the freedom went to my head and my exam results never matched my promise: the days went on a love affair, trying to write plays and forays into left-wing politics. Peter actually joined the Communist Party, an odd thing to do, it may seem, at that time in the Cold War, but what we sought were values that were neither those of our background nor the snobbisms and insincerities that still persuade southern middle-class Britons of their place in the world. When I say that I am still searching I sound naive even to myself, and I am not much cheered by the realisation that many other British artists and intellectuals have become mired in the same pursuit.

If Manchester United was the passion, any sort of football was of interest. Today, walking our dog in Hyde Park, I always watch the players there for their first touch and to see their left foot in action; in the 1940s I cycled from home to see the famous Preston Ladies at Hazel Grove. Sometimes a neighbour would take me with him to see Stockport County, our nearest League team, for whom early in the mid-50s we saw Alec and David Herd play together at inside forward, an extraordinary father and son combination; and on many a spring evening my cousin Donald Young and I walked up from his house, past mill lodges and with the moors in the distance, to watch Oldham Athletic Reserves in the Lancashire Combination. We had a comic hero, an outside left named Parnaby, who mostly fell over himself but sometimes produced a thunderclap, like the free kick he once drove through the Rossendale wall.

Many times I went from Cambridge to visit John Howarth, another school friend, older than me, who worked on the *Acton Gazette*. After Jean Ainslie, the wife

of the master who ran the school amateur dramatic
society, John's parents Jack Howarth and Betty
Murgatroyd were the first professional actors I knew, and
very glamorous to me. They were northern rep players
who had always lived in digs. They were at Colwyn Bay
for the war and then moved to Ealing to what was I
think their first actual home together. I hung on their
every reminiscence, and one of them still makes me
laugh. Jack, in the witness box in some courtroom drama,
said 'Yes' when he should have said 'No', destroying
thereby the entire plot of the play: he was bewildered
and finally incensed as the other actors improvised around
him. Later, Betty came into family money and they moved
to a big house in Deganwy, and later still Jack became
Albert Tatlock in *Coronation Street*. John stuck with the
journalism. He knew from his childhood that show-
business was rickety. I last saw him at the end of the
1970s, at Lord's, in an interval for rain during an England
versus Pakistan Test Match. He talked about Billy Foulkes
and his organisation of the United defence against corner
kicks.

John was a decent games player – he actually appeared
in goal a time or two for Colwyn Bay – and a good
judge of actors and footballers. The team nearest their
house in Ealing was Brentford, and we would walk
down to see Tommy Lawton, still deadly in the twilight
of his career, lead the forward line. He had a very clean
first touch and did not waste the ball. 'There you are,'
John would say. 'With Lawton it's either a goal or a
save.'

At all these games I stood up: apart from a wet Easter
Saturday on which my father took it into his head to
drive Peter and me to see United at Derby, I do not

remember having another seat at a football match until I was sent into press boxes in 1954.

Crowds then were rougher but more pleasant than they are today. They shoved mightily to leave the ground or get into the trains, and at half-time lines of men pissed against the perimeter wall at the uncovered Stretford End. There were jovial remarks about our obvious middle-class attire ('How's your Crombie overcoat then?') and sallies at the expense of ageing players ('He missed one on Saturday I could have wafted in with my cap!') but there was no hate. There were more conversations and a much more sporting attitude to the opposition's good play. When a great personality like the Charlton goal-keeper Sam Bartram made his last appearance at Old Trafford, pulling off, as Old International of the *Guardian* wrote, 'more saves from what seems an inexhaustible repertoire', he received a standing ovation.

Old working-class men from Salford, in caps and mercerised white cotton mufflers, would talk about the United team of 1908, and boys would be helped into positions of greater safety or visibility. In the more expensive covered standing areas at both Old Trafford and Maine Road, Jewish petty businessmen would dispense their mordant wisdom.

Nor was there venom between rival supporters. There had been very violent crowd behaviour before 1914, which is why people like my mother did not think that football was safe, but two wars had made a lot of young men wiser. I once saw Jackie Milburn open the scoring against United with a thunderbolt from nothing – actually a little reverse ball by Ernie Taylor – and all around us rough men began to sing 'Blaydon Races'. But the discussions which followed were amicable and pretty knowledgeable. Everyone had played football, if only in the street, and I think that they looked at it more dispassionately than people do now, and with less neurotic allegiances. People were depressed or elated by football results but they had seen slumps and wars and did not confuse a team's failure with the disasters of life itself.

Sectarian violence did linger in Belfast, where the Celtic club was shut down, and in Glasgow between Rangers and Celtic. Millwall had occasional trouble, and when I wrote for *Z-Cars* in the early 1960s and went to do research in Liverpool, our police contact Bill Prendergast always said that violence would return to Goodison Park. Modern football hooliganism is supposed to have flared first among Millwall supporters in 1967, but I saw Everton fans fighting at Old Trafford a year earlier and have always believed that they were the originators. It would be hard to prove: one would have to sift through a lot of magistrates court reports to see where the earliest arrests were made and who the people were.

If there was geniality in the Old Trafford crowd after 1948 there was also frustration and the sense that the point about United's classical football was obvious but unproven. This was heightened by the slow but undeniable decline of the England international team. The last years of the war saw two things: an England team that was used as a morale booster and in disrupted conditions was the only regular line-up, and the maturity of some extremely talented players. Manchester City's Frank Swift, for example, is one of the very few individuals to have changed the way the entire game is played, because he invented modern goalkeeping: how the keeper dominates the whole penalty area, and by creative clearances is the first line of attack as well as the last in defence. Matthews, Carter, Lawton, Mannion and Finney were five geniuses in one forward line, and ballplaying defenders like George Hardwick and Neil Franklin would be a sensation in today's football. Even after changes this team played brilliantly, and a case could be made that the famous 4–0 victory over Italy in Turin in 1948 was a higher-water mark than winning the World Cup in 1966.

A mere two years later England were put out of the 1950 World Cup by the United States, and during the early 1950s prestige friendlies against Argentina, a FIFA XI and, eventually, Hungary seemed to reveal vast gulfs in technique. I saw the Argentina and FIFA games on the Peterhouse Junior Common Room's flickering black-and-white television, and the Hungarian exile Kubala left an indelible impression. A tall, powerful man who drove dagger-like at the heart of the defence, he played – surprise, surprise – for Barcelona, and there were other virtuosi alongside him in the FIFA squad. But the point, in a sense the same as when we saw the Hungarians on TV in 1953, was that we had seen ballplayers and movement at Old Trafford that we believed to be as good as these exotics. Carey, after all, had captained the Rest of Europe against Great Britain in 1948, and Eire when they beat England at Goodison Park, before the Hungarians were called the first foreigners to win on English soil. His screw kick up the line, bent around opponents on its way to the winger, was extraordinary when one considers the weight of the old leather football and its capacity to absorb moisture. Charlie Mitten had been fantastic, and decades later revealed that when he was in Bogotá the Argentinians di Stéfano and Hector Rial had asked him to go with them to Real Madrid. Morris, for all that his career fizzled out, was a magician, and so was Henry Cockburn, even if he did look like a stunted figure from the cotton mills.

Above all, in its combined play that first Busby–Murphy side had that rarest of all qualities in a football team: an absolute balance of talents, so there is always something natural and instinctive at work that makes the play seem effortless and inevitable. This is the notion that makes a team aesthetically great, as well as hard to play against. It underlay all Murphy's thoughts, and like many things that are difficult to achieve its essence is simple. For argument's sake, the opposed qualities in footballers are left- or right-footedness, and the balance between skill and athletic power. Each individual has his own mixture, and a lucky handful, like Pelé or Ruud Gullit, are born with a balance at maximum level. So were Maradona and George Best, small men of unusual strength.

Expressed in terms of each player's dominant quality, United's 1948 W formation defence lined up like this:

GOALKEEPER

SKILL   POWER

POWER   STOPPER   SKILL

In front of them the forward line had attacking equivalents in:

SKILL   DIRECTNESS

DIRECTNESS   MIXTURE   SKILL

The skilful outside left Charlie Mitten had a weaker right foot and mostly held his position, but the others showed considerable movement, which perhaps compensated for the fact that ideally the skilled winger would have played in front of the power half, and the direct one in front of the skilled half, as happened in 1967 when the wingers were Connelly and Best. The idea is that when in the heat of the moment a player does what comes most naturally it will be complemented by the instincts and qualities of his adjacent colleagues. To assemble amid life's confusions a group for whom this will happen is very difficult, which is why natural balance is not the same thing as the drilled percentage football of teams like Liverpool, Hitzfeld's Borussia Dortmund, Bayern Munich and Mourinho's Chelsea, all of whom made deliberate decisions to weight the team in favour of its destructive power.

When FIFA banned the tackle from behind in 1994 they gave attackers the advantage, and 3–5–2 and 4–1–4–1 systems are the response. We are in a defensive era masquerading as sensible counter-attack, and because a five-man midfield inevitably duplicates power defenders the game can lose some of its beauty and rely more on athleticism.

Natural balance is fragile. It is a less pragmatic way to run a team, one that leans more to dreams than common sense, but once it has been experienced it is a touchstone, like a profound love affair. In the case of Busby and Murphy's first United it held for about a year.

At the same time it was agreeable in the mid-1950s to watch the team, not expect them to win anything but be aware that a great future was on the way. In May 1953 United won the inaugural FA Youth Cup with a team that included Colman, Edwards, Whelan, Pegg and Scanlon. Altogether they won it five times in a row and lifted the Zurich International trophy twice. Supporters realised that it was not just a question of a production line as opposed to individuals, but of a production line that included truly great players. I saw Bobby Charlton score a Youth Cup Final goal against Chesterfield, flicking the ball over his head, wheeling and smashing it into the top corner, that was as majestic as anything in his pomp; I saw Duncan Edwards cruise through opponents like a dreadnought, snake-hips Eddie Colman shuffle and swerve them onto their backsides, and David Pegg produce drag-backs like Puskás or Ronaldo. They were the days when one's youth would last for ever, it seemed, and life would give us all our due reward.

Editor's whim

I had expected after Cambridge to do National Service and was a bit flummoxed to be rejected on account of a perforated eardrum, product of my sickly early childhood, and the flat feet that have now collapsed entirely and give me the discomfort that the doctor calls wear and tear. The news was given to me over the telephone by my mother, who added in gloomy but self-satisfied tones, 'So now you'll have to find yourself a job.'

The job I wanted was that of playwright, but I was clearly not ready to proceed. My father was sceptical of the whole thing and hoped that time would bring me to my senses. He suggested that I work in the mill as a yarn tester and I agreed. I thought that it would buy me a year or so, and it did.

I would drive up to the mill with my father and walk back alone in the afternoon. The work, measuring each mule or ring-frame's yarn for the correct weight and tension, was mechanical and soon done. I had a role in an industrial process, and a social structure, that had scarcely changed since the end of the eighteenth century. I had the late afternoon to write and the week-ends and some evenings to follow United. Apart from the fact that I did not know how to be what I wanted, it was fine.

John Howarth had moved from Ealing to the *Oldham Chronicle*. I would see him on many Wednesdays, when I hitched a lift on a cotton-waste lorry to join the weekly family tea at my grandfather's. My grandfather was soon to die, aged eighty-nine, but we would continue to make the Wednesday pilgrimage to see my spinster aunt, who had lived with my grandfather, and my widowed uncle, who lived next door but one. On the day that Hungary beat England I popped into the *Chronicle* office. John had seen the game on TV. His first words were, 'We were told that their fullbacks were weak but they were hitting forty-yard passes.'

'Well, how could we have won,' I replied, 'with nothing creative at wing half?'

It was a very Jimmy Murphy-like remark, I now realise, made five years before I met him.

I did write, and fail to complete, many scraps of plays and short stories, and I wrote about football as well: research into its early history, and little essays about players

I admired. One evening on the TV football highlights I saw United's former winger Jimmy Delaney playing for Falkirk in a Scottish Cup replay. Time had cut his speed but not his ability to combine heroism with farce, and I sat up in bed and wrote three or four hundred words about him, just for myself. Within a month or two they had set my life on its course.

Even when my grandfather was near death my father would engineer family conversations of which the subject was my future. 'People who write history books don't make so thundering much, you know!' he would begin, and very soon they would all be at it. Later I would hear my father and mother grumble through it again in their bedroom, and it may well have been her squeaky little replies that persuaded him to stop booming and bestir himself. He somehow won me an abortive interview for a devilling job on the financial pages of the *Manchester Guardian*.

The man who saw me was Patrick Monkhouse, son of the old Manchester Gaiety Theatre playwright Allan Monkhouse, and we detested each other on sight. Years later I wrote a weekly column for the paper. This first brush was a disaster, but it did not deter my father. His pride was up, and another scheme was suggested to him by his friend Leonard Whitehead.

Uncle Leonard, as I called him, was a portly jovial character with steel-rimmed glasses and puckers in his cheeks where a Great War bullet had passed through them. He was a yarn agent in business on his own account, and he liked to do interesting favours. They brought him custom, I suppose. Once he came to our house with a warrant officer who had been aboard HMS *Exeter* at the Battle of the River Plate and who surely went down with her in the Java Sea, and he would take us to Belle Vue Zoo and the fireworks display, and sometimes to the speedway. He now announced that he had a friend named Mr Nicholson who could get me a job on the London *Evening Standard*. All I had to do was write to the editor stating that it was at the suggestion of Mr Nicholson. I did so and enclosed my Jimmy Delaney essay. A letter duly came back and summoned me to London to meet John Junor.

He sat in an overheated steel and glass cage and wore a short-sleeved powder-blue silk shirt. He was thirty-odd, I guess, and looked like the Bay City police chief as described by Raymond Chandler: a hammered-down heavyweight. I liked him at once, and he liked my Jimmy Delaney piece and said that if I wrote another one about a current star he would print it. As I left he waited until I reached the door, held up my letter and said, 'Who is this Mr Nicholson?'

'I've no idea,' I said.

'Neither have I,' he grinned.

But he was as good as his word and printed a piece about Tom Finney, the first thing I ever wrote for money, and a month or two later summoned me to London again. He had moved to the *Sunday Express* and would give me a weekly match to report.

Under the wry eye of his northern sports editor Ken Adam, who must have seen many an editor's whim in his day, I was sent on each subsequent week of that 1954/5 season rail vouchers and a press ticket. My first game was Bolton Wanderers versus Leicester City, and as I loitered under the stand before the game who should pass me, whistling to himself and jingling the change in his pockets, but my former United hero Johnny Morris, now the Leicester playmaker. In the press box Archie Ledbrooke and Henry Rose sat right behind me. When the Leicester left-winger Derek Hogg floated in front of us a spectator yelled, 'W. H. Smith born again!', a remembrance of one of Herbert Chapman's stars when he managed Huddersfield, and Archie Ledbrooke agreed with him in a lordly fashion. I was indeed on Olympus.

In the ensuing weeks I made many mistakes. Half the time I never knew how to organise my phone and reversed the charges when I wasn't supposed to. Once my report took so long to write that I found myself locked in the empty Hillsborough press box, and had to cross the snowy pitch and climb over a wall at the Leppings Lane End. On most occasions I was too nervous to speak to people or go for a drink in the boardroom, but every week I wrote the exact number of words, saw them appear under the byline Tom Ashley, and received my money through the post. And at Goodison Park, Anfield, Maine Road, Blackpool, Burnley, Bolton, Hillsborough, Bramhall Lane, Preston and Blackburn I had a crash course in the atmosphere and quality of football in the mid-50s.

Sometimes, on buses or at stations, I saw players on their way home, and was intrigued by the solitariness of the great Blackburn winger Bobby Langton or the edgy jokes and conceit of Sunderland's expensive line-up: the amazing Shackleton, the playboy Ken Chisholm, the big, brilliant cynical Scot George Aitken and their manager Bill Murray. I watched them in the buffet at Sheffield Victoria, a station that no longer exists, and I guessed then that Murray did not have Busby's sort of control over his team. Of course he hadn't. Had they not been gathered by a fortune in illegal payments?

★　　★　　★

At the end of the season the *Evening Standard* asked me to write a piece about the Manchester City versus Newcastle United Cup Final, and I said that City's deep-lying centre forward system would leave a gap into which Ron Scoular would drop his crossfield passes, which is what happened – although City might have overcome this had they not been reduced to ten men. The article was sent up the wire and appeared under my name in the Manchester *Evening Chronicle*, which gave me the idea to write to them, enclosing my cuttings, to ask for a job. I went into Manchester one afternoon without telling my parents, and was offered a place on the *Evening Chronicle* under the Kemsley Newspapers Graduate Trainee Scheme.

My mother's brother Uncle Fred, who was with the Lancashire Fusiliers at Gallipoli, and saw both Steve Bloomer and Denis Law, and thought Law the better player, said that the time after a young man gets his first job is the happiest in his life. It is an unreconstructed pre-1914 northern opinion that still holds not a little truth.

Trainee

Something like a dozen titles were published out of Kemsley's Withy Grove, and it was a humming, strip-lit, oil and piss and tobacco and sausage-sandwich-smelling place in which the machine-room and linotype men

were grotesquely overpaid, and the journalists thought
that the papers belonged to them. Under its editor Johnny
Goulden, a grey, sharp but not unkindly, spectacled little
man in dull three-piece suits, the *Evening Chronicle* was
engaged in a serious circulation battle with the *Manchester
Evening News*. One of Goulden's ploys was to reprint for
free in the *Chronicle* every small ad that appeared in
the *News*, and another was slip editions, that is to say
local pull-outs, for each surrounding town. Times were
exciting, and Withy Grove itself exuded legendary
memories: of Hulton's pre-1914 racing sheets, of horse-
drawn delivery vans racing up Market Street to be first
to the railway station, and of hardship in the 30s, when
out-of-work subeditors came with their own scissors and
paste and ruler and stood in a mob, hoping to be picked
for a night's casual work.

There was one other graduate on the paper, who wrote
about show business, and we were both regarded as
persons who could never be truly street smart, which in
my case was true, however much my mentors tried. The
news editor Bob Walker was an indecisive white-haired
man who liked to keep the staff in the office in case
there was an air crash: eventually there were two, both
out of our working hours. His deputy Harold Mellor,
however, was a classic. Once he sent me on a story about
a calf that had escaped for a few minutes on the way to
the abattoir. I handed in my piece and sat down.

'Mr Dewhurst!' came the cry.

I went to Harold's glass coop. He threw my pages back
at me.

'Do you mean to tell me,' he said, 'that nobody scattered for cover?'

Harold, a pot-bellied, chain-smoking, very friendly

bulldog, was also a master, on a slow summer news day, of readers' letters. His best, accompanied by an illustration from the paper's cartoonist, read, 'Dear Sir. When my sixteen-year-old daughter comes home late I put her across my knee and give her a hiding. Yours, Old Fashioned, Moss Side.' The ensuing response was most lively.

After a couple of months I was sent to Wigan, where the paper sold a four-page slip edition and maintained two other reporters and a photographer named Arnold Hall, who when we first shook hands said, 'I wasn't always a little fat man, you know.' Photographers, in those days of cumbersome equipment and glass plates, were free with corner-of-the-mouth advice and an essential part of the training, as was the sprightly little contest in Wigan itself between papers from Manchester, Liverpool and Preston. I lived in digs in Warrington Lane, near the house where George Orwell lodged when he researched *The Road to Wigan Pier*. The fire station and the borough police were between me and the milk bar where the journalistic community gathered of a morning, so I would do those calls on my way in. Once I rode on an appliance to a fire, and they trained a hose on a woman's blazing kitchen range, blasting its contents all over the room.

What was interesting about post-Orwell Wigan, I guess, was that it basked in full employment and the fruits of Labour's victories. Ostensibly it looked to the future, but in truth to the past. It did not want to change. It wanted to be allowed to be itself. Most of the apparent revolution of the 1960s was the capitalist market's response to that desire, and to the hedonism of secure young people with pay packets.

My return to the Manchester newsroom coincided more or less with the build-up to the arrival of commercial television. This was a big news event. There were to be two new studios in Manchester, and as the spare graduate assumed to know something about the arts I was seconded to the TV reporter. My good luck here cannot be overemphasised: through covering the start of Granada TV I came to know the people, including indeed my first wife, who would enable me to make a start as a scriptwriter. I also came within a whisker of my one and only big scoop as a reporter. I had a Cambridge friend whose father was a big player in London advertising and knew that Granada had made a secret and illegal deal to be subsidised by the London TV companies. In my naivety I put the story to the Granada Manchester press office, and when a ton of bricks descended on Bob Walker he knew that it was true but could not be proved. He commended me but was perhaps relieved. He was a hopeless day-to-day organiser but he did have a sophisticated mind. Other newspapers had a share in the offending companies. The story was out of our league and might even have been suppressed.

An advantage of this newsroom training was that I took days off on Saturday and could follow the football. In 1956 Manchester City won the Cup and the Busby Babes burst upon the world to win the First Division Championship by eleven points. This was a huge margin when it was two for a win and one for a draw. The win that clinched the title was against Blackpool, Stanley Matthews and all, in mud and rain before a crowd of 62,000. Johnny Doherty, he of the grumbles against the PLC, hit the bar with a diving header, and was the playmaker in the hole behind the rampant front men Taylor and Viollet.

At the start of the next season, in the autumn of 1956, Doherty lost his place to Billy Whelan, who a year later I saw parade the ball skills of the continental masters in a 3–0 defeat of Everton. It was this display, with its possession football, its physical power and its machine-like combination in both attack and defence, that persuaded me that here was not just an inspirational team but something historic, something built to dominate for a long time.

By then Johnny Goulden had transferred me from the newsroom to the sports table, and the best group of people I ever worked with.

Sports table

I used to watch them from the newsroom – on the far side of the metal tables and lockers, the typewriters up-tipped like wrecked armoured vehicles, the mess of paper and bins – through the cigarette smoke that at the end of the day hung in veils under the strip lights. I would stare at Alf Clarke, the legend of my boyhood, with his red face, his fishy eyes, his pipe, his sloping belly beneath a cardigan and a shiny suit. I would see the bald pate and sallow sunken cheeks of the sports editor Jack Smith as his lean frame stooped over the copy and he made swift decisions, and the hunched back of the owl-spectacled columnist

Arthur Walmsley, who likened Bobby Charlton to a bird on the wing. The others kept themselves to themselves but one could see that they were friends as well as effective colleagues, a paper within the paper, as it were, because they did indeed have their own football pink on a Saturday. But when I joined them I discovered that there were subtle divisions.

The core group, to which I was admitted, consisted of Jack, his deputy Ted Coghill, the chief sub Don Frame and Arthur Walmsley. What made them the inner group was that they were public-house buddies who would sit for hours and talk. They would be joined from time to time by Jack Wild, who had heavy spectacles and worked in small ads, and Charlie Hannigan, a Scotsman of white moutachios and some style, who was a group circulation executive. Charlie was a Glasgow Catholic acquaintance of Matt Busby, and Jack Wild had served in the Stockport Home Guard under my father, whom he regarded as a comic martinet but a man who would have been invaluable had the Germans actually landed.

Sometimes Jack Smith would cross the road to the Ship, a gloomy pub run by a man called Ernie, and take the page proof with him, so that if he was locked in during afternoon closing time he could make last-edition changes over the phone. The group would go after work to the Sugar Loaf, just up Withy Grove, a pub with superb wood and glass decorations and, like many in Manchester, entrances at front and back. Both these pubs were destroyed for the building of the Arndale Shopping Centre. When the necessity of going home loomed even for him, Jack would lead the way to the bar on Platform 18, Victoria Station. He lived at St Anne's, and would miss several trains while evaluating football tactics, rivalries in the Manchester City boardroom, or what could be done to get more money from Johnny Goulden and make our pages better. It wasn't that these men, all of whom had been in the war and valued peacetime, actually drank a lot, you understand, not like me and Bill Bryden and our National Theatre actors drank a lot twenty years later. It wasn't that they consumed numerous sandwiches and Scotch eggs and pickles along the way. It was that they talked and talked, about their job and about good writing and old journalistic ploys.

IT DIDN'T RAIN TODAY FOR FOLLOWERS OF THE EVENING CHRONICLE RACING SERVICE. IT RAINED PENNIES FROM HEAVEN was one of Jack's late edition racing puffs, and he gave an instant response when Johnny Goulden called the heads of the editorial departments to discuss the fact that because TODAY'S HOROSCOPE came up on the wire from London, and we were an evening paper, the day was over before most people came to read their stars.

'There's a very simple answer to that, Mr Goulden,' said Jack. 'Call it TOMORROW'S HOROSCOPE.'

Which they did that very afternoon.

The second sports sub, Ernie Bottoms, a bald man with a ripe Oldham accent, worked in a Fair Isle pullover with his sleeves rolled up. He had come from the *Daily Mirror* because his wife did not like him working nights, and his tabloid leanings were not entirely approved of. Not that Jack's men were above the lurid in the right place and time. I wrote a summer boxing series about the last bare-knuckle champion Tom Sayers, above one instalment of which Don Frame put the three-decker headline HELD OVER RED HOT COALS IN BATTLE FOR

MISTRESS. But this approach would not have done, say, for a match-saving half-century by Cyril Washbrook.

Ernie went home early to his wife and so, but more lugubriously, did Eric Todd, who covered Manchester City in the winter and Lancashire cricket in the summer. Jack Smith's relationship with Eric was civil but not intimate, and soon after Old International died at Munich Eric joined the *Guardian*. I can't remember whether it was for them or us that he wrote his great line 'If things go on like this, Manchester City won't have to buy players, they'll have to buy spectators.'

Jimmy Breen, and later Henry Tomlinson, wrote about rugby league, bluff fellows both of whom Jack respected, but they were not intimates, and neither were Bill Clarke, Alf's less torpid brother and editor of the *Sporting Chronicle,* who covered Bolton Wanderers and Bury, nor Claude Harrison, gentlemanly and much loved, who wrote about horse racing under the pseudonym Carlton.

A legendary freelance contributor was Jack Davies, who wrote about panel bowls, that professional game played on public-house greens with bookmakers in attendance: a folkloric sort of event that harked back to the sporting bucks of the Regency because the outstanding player was the one who could feign disaster. The odds would lengthen, his friends place the money, and the game be retrieved from the jaws of catastrophe. Jack Davies himself was a tall old man in the manner of L. S. Lowry and Vince Hayes, wearing a similar rain-battered coat and trilby. He gave his copy to the Wigan office, where the lads wound him up by reporting rumours that he was worth hundreds of thousands. 'There you are,' he would say. 'That's just how these things start.'

Because I had witnessed these ribbings I was adjudged an expert, and Arthur Walmsley, who had followed the bowling in his youth, would quiz me as to the value of Jack's printed forecasts. Were they real or an attempt to rig the betting? To this day I haven't the faintest idea.

There is a passing parade through every sports department, and Jack Smith could treat them all the same, from the lost, punch-drunk Jackie Brown, a former world champion, to the Australian cricketer Cec Pepper, who would blow in like a southerly buster hitting Sydney's beaches. Jack was a Catholic with high standards but an awareness of people's failings. He was quiet, amusing, direct and encouraging. He made everyone feel worthwhile: Ernie our typesetter, John Senior, who wrote the newsbills and sat at a table near ours looking into a tiled interior well, our copy boy Bracegirdle and Dick Sutton, ostensibly a linotype operator but actually the illegal bookmaker for the entire building.

Ted Coghill, bespectacled and serious, who ghosted Busby's articles in the pink, was the chief organiser of our visits to racecourses and the daily bets, although, of course, on the day that Claude Harrison's treble actually came up at something like 143–1 we didn't have our steady penny each on it. Arthur Walmsley rarely gambled but was the great raconteur and dispenser of advice, the *consigliere* of the Mafia family, who under his chuckles and his eye for the ludicrous was a romantic who believed that sport was a metaphor for something noble. He worried about things, and in the end his health buckled and he gave up journalism. Jack, too, was an idealist, but more pragmatic. As part of the circulation war he sponsored athletics meetings in Manchester and could make an illegal payment with the best of them. And his artistry with an expenses form was exquisite. But that was his operating cash. His salary went straight to his wife Agnes.

My work on the sports table, where I sat next to Ted Coghill with my back to the room and the main subs table, was a mixture of writing and subediting. I was banned from the St Helens ground (so far as I know the ban has never been lifted) for a series called 'The Most Hated Team in the Rugby League' and for the pink I wrote a column about sport on TV. I wrote for Manchester City's wing half Roy Warhurst and their manager Les McDowall when the regular ghosts were off sick, and on Saturdays I covered a match, rugby league as often as soccer. We took our days off in the week and would go to the race meetings at Manchester, Chester and Haydock. One of the best things was that everyone's wives liked each other, and there was a lot of social contact. My first wife loved horses and was good at picking winners in the paddock.

Towards the end of the 1957 football season Eric Todd went on his holidays to be ready for the cricket, and on the last day Jack sent me to Birmingham with Manchester City to cover the game for the pink. I had to travel with the team and dictate a running report over an open phone line. The trick was to speak no more words than the space allocated could carry.

Les McDowall I knew but he was away on a scouting mission ('More likely nightclubs in London,' said Arthur Walmsley), and the train party consisted of the team, the trainer Laurie Barnett and two directors, one of them Fred Jolly, a shopkeeper who to Arthur Walmsley typified the difference between Manchester City and United.

Arthur had two stories about Jolly, both of which seemed exaggerated, but after sitting next to him on the train and in the cavernous railway hotel dining room I became convinced that they were true.

Jolly was a wizened little white-haired man who offered me a Fox's Glacier Mint from a paper bag, and the first story was about the team arriving at Newcastle station. Fred panicked, opened the wrong door, and contrived to spill the skip containing the playing kit on to the tracks. The second story was set in Gloucester Road, London, where City stayed at Bailey's Hotel. There was an ornamental garden outside the Tube station, and around this garden a low wall. Fred came out of Bailey's for the Tube and fell over the wall. A porter rushed out of the station to pick him up. Fred put his hand into his pocket and by way of thanks held out his clenched fist. The man touched his forelock and accepted the tip. It was, of course, a Fox's Glacier Mint.

At childhood heart Arthur was a City supporter, but his knowledge of the men in the boardroom made him worry about the club's future in a changing world. And indeed, in the end, the sacking of the wise old pilot Joe Mercer and Malcolm Allison's second term as manager can be seen now as mistakes whose consequences have still not finally unravelled. Happily, on that day in 1957 City managed a fighting 3–3 draw with Birmingham City in hazy spring sunshine, and my report was adjudged a success.

This was of course the spring in which United chased the treble of League, Cup and European Cup, and Matt Busby's fame spread beyond the football pages when his life story was serialised in the Sunday *Empire News*.

★   ★   ★

In the late summer of 1956, just before that defining moment when the Royal Court Theatre put on Osborne's *Look Back in Anger*, Busby had urged the United board to defy the advice of the Football League and its narrow-minded secretary Alan Hardaker, and compete in the European Cup. Their decision was more than justified by the extraordinary drama of the matches and the interest they aroused.

What made such extra games possible were air travel and the spread of floodlights, although to start with there were none at Old Trafford, and United played their first three ties at Maine Road. The potential of night games against high-level opposition had been shown by the friendlies which Wolves played against Honved, the Hungarian club that fielded most of the country's international team, and by others like the one in which Inter Milan famously thrashed West Ham at Upton Park. But the decisive thing was serious competition, and here United's vision was equal to that of Gabriel Hanot, the editor of the French sports paper *L'Equipe*, who conceived the European Cup.

United won a tight 2–1 victory against Anderlecht in Belgium but ran riot in the home leg and scored ten. In the next breathless round they went three up against Borussia Dortmund and saw the Germans pull two back in the second half, and then held on for a goal-less draw in Dortmund. The first quarter-final leg took place in an afternoon snowstorm in Bilbao, and I remember the excitement on the sports table as Alf's report came over in bits and pieces. In the end United lost 5–3 and would need to score three in the second leg.

It was a legendary crowd-roaring night. Arthur and

Alf were in the press box and the rest of us on the terrace behind the goal. Don Frame bounced up and down with his pipe still in his mouth as United crashed in the goals. None of us had seen football drama like it.

Soon after that match, which took place on 6 February, a year to the day before the Munich crash, Old Trafford got floodlights. For one early night game United experimented with an all-red strip. When Alf Clarke announced this he stole the pre-war name for the Salford rugby league team. He began his piece, 'They'll be calling Manchester United the Red Devils next,' recoining thereby the phrase that has achieved world currency and seen a little devil replace the city arms on the club crest.

The League and Cup double had last been achieved by Aston Villa in 1897, and the emotional build-up to all United's games was now intense. Before the European semi-final against Real Madrid, Arthur was sent to Spain to interview Alfredo di Stéfano and analyse the champions, and I went to Blackburn (changing trains at Accrington, which still looked like 1897) to interview a Catholic priest.

The club that became Real Madrid had been founded in the early 1900s by young English seminarists, and this old man was one of the originals. He had photographs of himself and his friends in their football strip and lounging in their cassocks, and he gave me sherry and biscuits. When I held out my glass for a top-up he poured half of it into my shoe. I was given a lift back to Manchester by a young priest from Salford who told me how worried they all were about Albert Scanlon's spiritual welfare and how Busby had asked the fathers to have a word. As I recall it, a young lady and perhaps another player or two were involved, but whatever Albert had or had not done there was no need to worry about him. When I met him a year later it was clear that he is one of God's innocents; and although after football his life has been ordinary, his dignity is timeless.

That a priest would say these things to a reporter, and that the reporter would tell his sports editor, who would smile, shake his head and do nothing, is in the present day almost unimaginable. Less so the hot water that we got ourselves into with Bob Walker for running the Madrid story before our sister paper the *Blackburn Telegraph*, who had told him about the old seminarist in the first place. Jack mollified him with Cup-tie tickets. Not that Bob ever went himself. It was largesse for a friend outside journalism.

United were beaten 3–1 in Madrid, the limits of their experience exposed, although the result did serve to whip up hopes of another miracle. Alas, it was not to be. The sports staff stood at the Stretford End in evening sunshine, a few feet away from where Kopa, Hector Rial and di Stéfano cut up United. My heart still jumps at the memory of Rial, unexpectedly in space, snapping his shot against the crossbar. Years later I realised from his obituaries that when he did that he was forty years old. Madrid went two up, and although United equalised on the night they were out.

A couple of days later a girl came into the office and said that the Real outside left Gento had promised to marry her. Jack put his arm around her and took her to the lift and said that he would do what he could, but nothing more was heard of it.

In the ensuing weeks United won the League again and I sat in the Old Trafford press box for the first time, in Alf's seat where our direct line was installed, to report another victory in the Youth Cup Final. How could one know that it would be the last until 1964? On the day of the actual Cup Final I drew the correct score Aston Villa 2, United 1 in the office sweep, and wrote picture captions for the pink. 'Dream's end' said one of them, and there was a sourness about us, because United's goal-keeper Ray Wood had been taken off injured after a collision he should never have invited. A few days later I met Matt Busby for the first time.

The final had been played in sunshine, but the weather broke and the evening of the *Chronicle*'s drinks party for Matt and the players was wet and cold enough for Johnny Doherty to wear his camel hair overcoat, although being Johnny he might have worn it anyway. He was back in the reserves by then, and soon to be transferred to Leicester, where knee trouble finished him. It is an indication of how Matt regarded the event, I suppose, that there were no more than six players present and none of them, so far as I remember, important first-teamers. Not that I would remember, because Matt's charisma was all that was required, and it was immense. There was a knot of people around him in that gloomy reception room, decorated in the 1920s to express the power of a press barony, and the light outside the tall leaded windows was fading. Jack turned and made space to introduce me. Matt shook my hand and smiled and the conversation resumed. I did not meet him again for some ten months, when he at once remembered my name and who I was.

Because I was the youngest member of the sports staff and had no children to worry about I took my 1957 summer holiday late. We went to Ireland and added on some working days to enable me to write about Shamrock Rovers, United's first opponents in the new European Cup campaign. I saw the first leg at Dalymount Park, which United won 6–0 with a display of superiority like those that crushed the modern Brondby. In the next round they beat Dukla Prague smoothly enough, but in the League their rhythm stuttered. It was during that long spell of Tommy Taylor's poor form, when Busby kept him in the team because the other players relied on his spirit.

If that was an old-fashioned judgement of men, what happened next was ruthless decision-making and the first use in England of the modern squad system. Busby bought Harry Gregg for £25,000, at that time a world record fee for a goalkeeper, and dropped Berry, Jones, Whelan and Pegg and brought in Charlton, Blanchflower, Morgans and Scanlon. The result, from late December onwards, was a run of victories.

At this stage of the season I reported early-round FA Cup ties: one at Tranmere, where the press box was on the top deck of a superannuated bus, and one at Wigan, where I was met by Cyril Dickinson, a craggy but mild man old enough to be my father. I had known Cyril as a local reporter, and he now announced that he was my copy boy.

'But where's the phone?' I said.

Cyril handed me a goodish-sized stone.

'What?' I said.

He explained that there were no phones in the press box but that I would be sitting above an entrance. I would write my copy, wrap the paper round the stone and drop it down to him. He would throw back the stone and take the paper to the phone. This happened with fifty words after half an hour, fifty at half-time and twenty-five more at ten past four. It was the last time I saw Charlie Mitten, who was playing for Mansfield.

In the third round United had a dodgy win at Workington, where Dennis Viollet came to the rescue with a hat-trick, and in the fourth they were drawn against Alf Ramsey's Ipswich Town. Jack sent me down to watch Ipswich in action and if possible have a word with Ramsey. I introduced myself to him in the board-room and asked if this was the eleven that he hoped to play against United. He smiled and said, 'What time's your train back?' He was awkward, and his question seems more dismissive now than it did then, when I ascribed most things to my own shyness. But I saw the flicker of conceit in his eye, an instant of both steel and amusement, and although I admired him as a guerrilla leader I did not like him.

I saw the ensuing Cup tie because my appointed match was postponed. United won 2–0 but not before Ramsey's system had sprung a few surprises. He had an outside left named Leadbetter who could hit long diagonal passes like David Beckham did in his heyday, and other forwards who ran late from the deep. The novelty of it was to carry them through the divisions to the Championship. In that Old Trafford tie they hit the post early on and if they had scored might well have won, but when the ballplay flowed they had no answer. Ramsey's system was a brilliant trick to cover limited resources; the only manager to have done that sort of thing better is Brian Clough.

United's opponents in the Quarter-Final of the European Cup were Red Star Belgrade, and somehow

Jack got me in with them. I was at Old Trafford on the night they went to inspect the floodlights, when I stood next to the United captain Roger Byrne and was amazed to realise that he was not very tall, and on the Saturday before the midweek tie I travelled on the Red Star bus when they went to watch United at Leeds.

It was an agonising journey because I arrived late for the rendezvous at the Midland Hotel and had no time to go for a piss. I spent much of the journey doubled up on the back seat of the coach, shoved past people to get off, and ran inside to the gents. They must have thought I was crazy. On the way out of the gents, at the foot of the stairs that led up from the main entrance, I bumped into Matt Busby.

'Hello, son,' he said, and asked me what I was doing there. When I told him, he asked if the Red Star party seemed satisfied with the arrangements. He was going to the dressing room for a last word but behaved as though I was the one person in Leeds he had come to see, and had all the time in the world to do so. What a difference, I thought, to Ramsey.

The Leeds match was a draw which proved nothing, although it was the first time that I saw Jack Charlton play, and on the bus back the great inside forward Rajko Mitic was the joker, and I sat next to the Red Star manager Milorad Pavic. He was a handsome greying man who spoke good English because he had been in a prisoner-of-war camp with British soldiers. One of them was a former Bradford City player named Jimmy Lovery, and Pavic invited him to Manchester and asked me to meet him. Lovery was a cheery, bow-legged rolling little working-class man not absolutely at ease in the luxury hotel, but their reunion was joyous.

The evening of the match was tense and foggy, and Red Star went ahead when their tall and elegant outside left Kostic chipped Harry Gregg from a long way out, a classic European goal, but passion and storming attacks gave United a 2–1 advantage.

In their next game United beat Bolton Wanderers 7–2, one of their most satisfying victories, it always seemed to me, because Bolton epitomised the hard-running, hard-tackling physical power game that to this day is the core and curse of so much British football. To have them slaughtered was marvellous. The game before the trip to Belgrade was away to Arsenal, that last classic exhibition in which the Babes twice went up a gear to win 5–4. After Belgrade they would be at home to Wolves, the League leaders, and we were sure that in this vein of form they would win and storm to the title. Herbert Chapman was the only manager to have won three successive titles, and we suspected that this was a yardstick against which Matt chose to measure himself.

Saturday morning on the sports table was always a time to itself, a lull before the storm, and I was there at about ten o'clock when Alf Clarke phoned in from London, not to the typists to confirm the team for the Arsenal game, but to Jack with the news that the United director George Whittaker had just been found dead in his hotel room. 'It looked,' said Alf, 'as though he got up for a piss and collapsed.' Jack smiled and ran the story, and the team wore black armbands.

Arthur was the only one of us to have properly met George Whittaker, although we all knew what he looked like from team photos: an Edwardian-looking buffer with a walrus moustache. None of us had an inkling of the importance of his death. How could we? But a week or two before, in United's hidden boardroom warfare, Whittaker had vetoed the appointment of Matt's man Louis Edwards. An impediment had been removed to a future that would now happen.

PART TWO
Munich

Some daft woman on the line

Alf Clarke was not the most intelligent or expressive of men, and Jack Smith sometimes opined that when he was given the United job in 1928 it was because they were no-hopers and it seemed a good place to hide someone. Tom Jackson, who covered United for the *Evening News*, was a brighter sort of person altogether, but he was not, unlike Alf, a popular hero despite it all. More than once I saw Alf in cafes eating a solitary evening meal. He was said to have a stand-offish relationship with his wife and son, and to have a doom-laden alliance with a woman whom Arthur Walmsley always called the Black Widow. He had been a talented amateur footballer in his day and still held the goal-scoring record for the Manchester Wednesday League; and at a low ebb in United's fortunes, when one of the travelling players fell ill, Alf had actually turned out for them against Grimsby Town.

Or so it was said. It was also averred, vehemently by Alf himself, that it was due to him that United had escaped relegation to the Third Division. In the critical 1934 clash at Millwall, Alf claimed, he had stood up in the press box and shouted, 'Give it to so-and-so!' They did, and so-and-so scored the first goal. Whether this is true or not, and whether a shout from the press box could be heard on the pitch at the Den, I cannot say. But it deserves to be true, because United were Alf's life, and he was the unlikely, ponderous, ungrammatical harbinger of their greatness. He always wrote that United would achieve a supreme position, and they did. In 1953, after he had been with them for twenty-five years, the board gave him a gold watch.

How many of their secrets he knew but did not divulge to his sports editors is anybody's guess. But since he was close to Louis Rocca and Walter Crickmer, and attended annual general meetings as a shareholder, I imagine that he knew a good few, which would account in part for the punctiliousness of his relations with the sports table. Alf always observed the letter of the formalities: his copy may have varied in length but it was always on time; he always did what he said he would do, and he was always in contact. When the northern press stars went with Matt to see Real Madrid in Nice, an occasion on which Matt is said to have handed out pocket money, Alf reported every move. There is a photograph of them all on the Promenade des Anglais, laughing and confident like aristos of a provincial old world.

'Fucking in the streets to music,' Alf's phone description of the Dortmund Oktoberfest, became an office classic, and so did his complaint during the Red Star game that 'there was some daft woman on the line'. There was trouble in receiving his running report because the Yugoslavs had inadvertently linked two press box phones together, and Alf seems to have been the only person not to realise that the 'daft woman' was Tom Jackson of the *Evening News*. When the phone problems were solved it became clear that the match itself was a dramatic affair. United ran up a three-goal lead but were brought back to 3–3 by what the next morning's reports described as dubious free kicks. Months later, when they could talk about it, people like Bill Foulkes and Viollet and Albert Scanlon said that for much of the game United played splendid football.

Thursday afternoon

We were subbing the last features pages of the Saturday pink when Alf rang from Munich to say that the return flight was delayed by snow and they might have to travel overland. When I was writing I sat on the writers' table and when I was subbing I sat with the subs, which made it crowded, five of us around the smaller of the two tables, but we had more phones and the pneumatic message tubes that sent up the copy. John Senior had written his newsbills and gone home, and it was almost dark outside, and a nasty afternoon, when Alf rang again to say that having made two aborted take-offs the plane was about to try for a third. Jack had to lean over and disentangle cords to speak to him.

This phone call led to the final delay, when the plane doors were shut but opened again because a head count revealed one missing. Alf took his place amid ironic cheers.

Other calls were coming in, and after what seemed like a couple of minutes since Alf had spoken to Jack, someone rang from Kemsley House in London and said that there were unconfirmed reports that United's plane had been in an accident. Soon after that, stuff began to come in over our own wire machines. The plane had failed to lift off, been torn in two when it hit a building at the end of the runway and burst into flames.

I have no narrative memory of the next few hours, but what we had to do was get the paper out. Edition time. Stop-press if too late. Ted Coghill, a goalkeeper in his amateur soccer days, said, 'There you are, you see, goal-keepers!' when it was obvious that Gregg and Ray Wood had survived. Wilf McGuinness, held back in Manchester by an injury, came in with a friend, a man who was a driver on another newspaper, and sat at John Senior's table with tears in his eyes. We gave him cups of tea. I can't remember what jobs I did except at the end, when I wrote up the lists of who was dead and who was not. I headed them 'Saved', 'Believed saved' and 'These were aboard'. At first there were conflicting identifications but it was soon clear to us that all the journalists were dead, except for Frank Taylor of the *News Chronicle* and a *Daily Mail* photographer, Peter Ellyard, and his assistant. The mighty Frank Swift was dead, and Walter Crickmer, and the trainer Tom Curry, and Jimmy Murphy's assistant Bert Whalley, and Willie Satinoff, a raincoat manufacturer and figure on the sporting scene whose presence on the plane we did not understand but were too dulled to question. In fact, of course, he was Matt's other choice for a director, and must have been invited after Louis Edwards was vetoed but before George Whittaker died.

Seven players were dead: Byrne, Taylor, Colman, Pegg, Whelan the studious-seeming dribbler, stolid Mark Jones and Geoff Bent, the reserve fullback with a distinctive crouching style. I suppose I thought that the ones who had survived would reappear at once on the field, or perhaps I was too young to take in an enormity that I had not actually witnessed. But what I thought, and what we all said to each other, even when we were subbing that day's late edition, was that this was not the end. The dream would go on. The beautiful football would conquer, because it was the soul of our city.

In the days that followed there was gloom everywhere, black drapes and wreaths and handwritten epic poems in shop windows. There was a service in the cathedral and Barbirolli conducted the Halle in 'Nimrod', the musicians' traditional tribute to dead colleagues. But there was never despair, because what the city mourned were the dead servants of an ideal, and they were not thought to have lived in vain.

That Thursday, 6 February, was supposed to be the night of the press ball, for which we all had tickets, but nobody mentioned it. I went home to the rooms that my first wife and I rented before we were married. She was crying, but I don't think I did, not at the time, not literally. I did not cry until twenty-five years later, when I was living in the Pyrenees with my second wife, and I wrote an article about Munich for the *Radio Times*. I sat up late to finish, at a marble-topped table in a room with a big wood fire, and I realised how far I had travelled and to what uncertain purpose, and when I came to describe Tommy Taylor, the leader of the line, I could not. I started to weep, and I did not stop for half an hour.

Uphill finish

Jimmy Murphy missed Munich because he was with the Welsh international team, but he flew there next day. The week that followed was the week of the funerals, when a line of limos saw Henry Rose to his kosher rest, and the *Express* put up the banner headline HE WAS THE SPORTS KING OF THE NORTH; when the bodies of the players lay in state in the Old Trafford gymnasium; when the Black Widow tried to reach Alf's coffin, and Arthur Walmsley steered her away; when Matt lay in the oxygen tent in Munich, and Duncan Edwards flickered into consciousness, saw Jimmy at his bedside and whispered his last words: 'What time's the kick-off on Saturday?'

It was also the week that I was booked to tour the northern racing stables with Claude Harrison and a photographer. Claude had established this ritual over a decade and more: the train to Darlington, the local taxi driven by an ex-jockey, the pub at Middleham, the taxi to Malton and the pub run by another old jockey named 'Flipper' Dyson, the father of Terry Dyson, who played outside left in Tottenham's double-winning team of 1962. 'Flipper' came from the fact that he never used actual swear words. I had done the trip the year before, and wrote little features to accompany Claude's review of the equine talent.

This year I spotted a coat, a green wasp-waisted fur-collared masterpiece worn by an old man riding work at Malton for Charles Elsey. It turned out that the man was Billy Bullock, who in 1901 had ridden Signorinetta, the 100–1 freak winner of the Derby; later he went to Berlin, where a grateful owner had given him the coat. That was my best story, but what always fascinated me were the personalities of the trainers and head lads, and the rituals of their world.

Twenty years later I knew Lord Killanin, the president of the International Olympic Association, who was my theatre colleague's father-in-law, and he told me that his stepfather, who lived on Newmarket Heath, had once warned him most severely: 'Michael, you don't bring jockeys into the house!' That was in the late 1920s, and in the 50s it was not much better for journalists, although Claude, with his chuckle and his diffident natural grace, was allowed in some.

The glorious Neville Crump both had us in his house and spent a second evening with us in the pub. Sam Hall was a hugely overweight vernacular character from a sporting print, whereas Colonel Lyde one could very well imagine at the head of his regiment in the Peninsular War. He trained Quorum, who had run second to the great Crepello in the Guineas, and whom we saw that year snapping and sexually charged in his stall. Gerald Armstrong, who trained the ordinary racegoer's favourite stayer Morecambe, was shy and enthusiastic, like an elderly schoolboy, and Rufus Beasley, whose wife had run off with a stable boy, was a foxy man in an uncared-for house who specialised in Ascot raiders. Dick Peacock, nephew of the late Matt, who in 1945 had trained Dante, the last northern winner of the Derby, had a marvellously sexy wife, at the sight of whom our photographer's eyes bulged. She talked to Claude about staying at the Savoy, and London nightclubs, and his little replies were perfect: one would have thought him an habitué.

The previous year the sports table had enjoyed one of its best betting coups when Elsey's Babur won the Lincoln at 25–1. This year we stood at the top of the famous uphill finish to Elsey's gallops, and Babur and his pacemaker came thudding and snorting past us. Then we caught the train at Northallerton. Claude fell asleep and snored. At that time he was about sixty. His wife had died young, leaving him with two little girls, and he married her sister. They lived near us, facing Kersal Moor, and later my children went to infants' school with his grandchildren. When Claude died Kersal church was packed and the startled Vicar said that Mr Harrison was clearly most respected in his profession. At this the congregation of jockeys, tipsters, hack journalists, bookmakers, a few genuine toffs and locals who would have been shocked by what Claude could tell about the great Steve Donoghue's riding contracts, or which horses Charlie Smirke was supposed to have stopped on the arm and which he didn't, all smiled, because they knew that his acquaintance really had made their lives a little warmer.

Norbreck Hydro

When I returned from North Yorkshire to the office, Johnny Goulden and Jack offered me Alf's job. I accepted, ten years after I had read the pink in the milk bar and laughed at the journalese. I spent a day or two writing my racing features and on the Monday of the following week stayed with Jack Smith at St Anne's. He and his wife and I polished off a bottle of Tia Maria on the train, after which she cooked an excellent dinner. She was a dark woman, almost Mediterranean, but their tall, grave daughter was like Jack.

Next morning we went to the Norbreck Hydro, on the cliffs above Blackpool's North Shore. It was a classic seaside period-piece hotel with a golf course attached, at once friendly, a bit tired, comfortable and redolent of the years between the wars. If my family went to Blackpool, which they didn't very often because it was vulgar, they ate in the grill room of the Imperial, on the promenade in the middle of the town. The Hydro, I suspect, was at once too racy and too dull: dirty weekends, golf bores and, in winter and the midweek, dragons, as my father called widows and spinsters of a certain age.

In short, and considering that after a ten-minute trip the team bus could deposit everybody at the Tower to see the all-in wrestling, it was a perfect hotel for a football team, and I had been there before to ghost an article for the Manchester City manager Les McDowall. McDowall, a combination of the manse and the low life, was a fascinating character who might well have been created by his fellow Scot Robert Louis Stevenson. It was at the Hydro that I saw him grip the wrist of a waiter who was pouring cream over his fruit salad to ensure a continued flow, yet really he was fastidious. He had a contempt which he did not disguise for the fact that Don Revie's name had become attached to the deep-lying centre forward plan which he, McDowall, had devised, and in which the wing half Ken Barnes was just as important.

Jimmy Murphy had spirited the United players to the Hydro as soon as he could after the crash, and Jack and I awaited him in the corridor that ran behind the big glass-fronted rooms overlooking the sea. Various players passed us, and one of them, Fred Goodwin, told me later that when he saw me in my brown cord jacket he thought I was the hotel violinist. Then this man appeared, of about my own height, almost plump, quick little feet, a blazer and flannels, an air of stress and energy and impatience, a sandpaper voice and cheery warmth.

'Jack! How are you, my old pal?'

We were introduced. Keith Dewhurst. Jimmy Murphy. He gripped my hand and elbow. His hooded eyes blazed into mine and he said, 'Never mind criticism! What we need is support!'

He had already brought United's 1948 goalkeeper Jack Crompton from Luton to be the trainer, and one of the kindliest people in the Manchester United family, and signed Ernie Taylor from Blackpool. Taylor was a Geordie and had played for Newcastle and Blackpool, where he was the playmaker and the real architect of victory in the 'Matthews Cup Final' of 1953. He was small and solid, a neat dribbler and an accurate, imaginative passer. He had one England cap, won in the debacle against Hungary, but was a far better player than many who had been regular internationals. Jimmy brought him to scheme, and to hold the side together.

On the afternoon of the first match after Munich, the fifth-round Cup tie against Sheffield Wednesday, Jimmy landed Stan Crowther from Aston Villa, because without Edwards, Colman and the injured McGuinness, he needed a wing half to complement Fred Goodwin. The Football Association waived the fact that Crowther was Cup-tied, and he is the only player, certainly in modern times, to have played for two clubs in the same FA Cup campaign. Crowther had played very well in Villa's Cup Final win over United, but it cannot be said that he was a successful buy, which was more his own fault than anyone else's. He was a Brummie, tall, curly-haired, a sharp dresser in Italian-style suits. He was opinionated, quick-tempered and had a chip on his shoulder, and he never bought into the United myth. Footballers perforce try to get on with one another, but Stan did not in the end fit in, nor particularly want to: all of which was still to be revealed.

It was before the Sheffield Wednesday game that Jimmy Murphy gave his greatest team talk. He had intended it to be a big analysis but all he managed to say was, 'Play hard for yourselves, for the players who are dead, and for the great name of Manchester United . . .' Then he broke down and Jack Crompton said, 'Come on, then, lads,' and they walked out and boarded the bus.

Sheffield Wednesday

Sheffield Wednesday were a decent team with some gifted players, among them Albert Quixall, who later joined United, and Tony Kay and Peter Swan, who lost their careers in the match-fixing scandal of the 1960s; but a tornado of emotion settled over Old Trafford that night, and it is difficult in retrospect to see how Wednesday could have avoided their 3–0 defeat. The match was an extraordinary event of which I remember almost nothing: the crowd, most of all, some of them halfway up the floodlight pylons, and their noise and energy; the scarves with black diamonds against the names of the dead; the famous programme with no names on the team sheet; the impression that the lights gave of everything having been magnified and speeded up. Of the play I remember the curve on the ball when Shay Brennan scored direct from a corner, and his characteristic stooped hesitation before he stabbed it into the net for his second. I did a running report for a special stop-press edition and was still writing my think-piece for the morning when we rejoiced with our wives in the Cromford Club and Ernie Taylor came in, grinning, and we all shook his hand.

Then I was told to take one of my accumulated days off and went to London to meet the director William Gaskill, at that time an assistant at the Royal Court

Theatre in what were the days of its glory. He still remembers that when he asked me about the Sheffield Wednesday game, all I said was, 'The emotion was immense.' After our talk, which began a lifelong friendship, we walked out of the theatre and into Sloane Square, where a newsbill attached to a tree said: DUNCAN EDWARDS DEAD.

How good the dead giant was is a question very hard to answer. Strictly speaking, Taylor, Colman, Whelan and indeed Dennis Viollet all had more creative football brains, just as David Pegg had more skill with the ball. What made Edwards unique were his unfazed temperament and his balance, which delivered the full power of an awesome physique when and where he wanted it. There was little of the stretching which led Roy Keane to injuries as well as fouls. Edwards scored thunderous goals for England from the centre forward position, had a slashing crossfield pass and was a majestic defender. He could be as effective as Roy Keane but was still developing, in particular his confidence to dwell on the ball and change the tempo. Heaven knows what he might have become. The only comparable physical presence, I suppose, has been that of the rugby player Jonah Lomu.

As for the Babes as a team, it seems reasonable to say that they could have dominated English football for ten years, as Ferguson's teams did in the 1990s, because they were essentially a modern squad. How that squad would have held together after the abolition of the maximum wage in 1961 it is impossible to say but it is hard to believe that Busby would not have found a way. What is certain is that they were the most machine-like of United's great teams, the players having been drilled in what to do since they were very young. They could go up a gear when they needed to, and depending on personnel they exhibited the balance that was Murphy's perpetual quest.

Foulkes was a power fullback, with in front of him a scheming half in Colman, and in front of him a striking winger in Berry. Byrne was a ballplaying fullback, with in front of him the power of Edwards and the skill of Pegg. Inside Pegg, Viollet was a mixture of schemer and striker, and inside Berry, Whelan was a dribbler. At centre forward Taylor had both power and intelligence and was very good in the air. If there is a modern centre forward he resembled in his physique, suppleness and comfort on the ball it is Patrick Kluivert, except that Taylor was about twenty times more energetic. When Jackie Blanchflower was at centre half there was ballplay from that position too.

The Babes never had quite the underlying mystery of the teams of 1948 and 1967, but they were intended, I think, to be more practical: to dominate hard seasons in all weathers, a machine into which different players could be slotted according to form and situation. That this seemed just about to happen was not the least part of the loss.

PART THREE
On the Road

Politics

George Whittaker's death had come less than a year after that of another United director, Dr McLean, described to me by Jimmy Murphy as the most one-sided football spectator that he and Matt Busby had ever known. In his eyes United did no wrong, never played badly and never deserved to be beaten. In the end Matt and Jimmy became collectors, as it were, of the good doctor's comments, so much so that on the day McDowall's Revie-plan Manchester City thrashed United 5–0 at Old Trafford Busby did his best to raise the spirits of the demoralised troops and then left the dressing room to Jimmy because he wanted to dash to the boardroom to hear what excuses Dr McLean could find. He duly went up to him and said, 'Well, Doctor?'

'Well, Matt,' came the reply. 'What we saw today were two bad teams.'

The deaths left United with a board of only three directors: Hardman, James Gibson's son Alan and William Petherbridge. On the day after the Munich crash they met at Alan Gibson's house in Bowdon, a well-off residential suburb beyond Altrincham, and co-opted Matt's previously vetoed nominee Louis Edwards.

There was no guarantee at this stage that Busby would

recover from his injuries, and if there was respect between himself and Harold Hardman there was no great liking. When Busby joined United, James Gibson had agreed that he would have a free hand in management. They are said to have had a spat or two in private but it was Harold Hardman who, as far back as 1945, had commented in public on some of Busby's decisions. Busby confronted him and asked for the item 'Interference by Directors' to be placed on the agenda of the next board meeting. Hardman was forced to back down.

Alan Gibson, a gentle, not very handsome and hesitant sort of man, like a sickly schoolboy who does not seem to have been favoured with anything – except that in Alan's case he had money – had been told by his late father to support Mr Busby at all times. It is a remarkable testimony to Busby's influence that even when for all they knew he was dying, the board voted for his man Louis Edwards.

It must have been obvious to Hardman, a man in his seventies, that Edwards, forty-three years old and at the height of his powers, was there not just to nullify him but to take over if possible in the long run. That the situation was delicate is emphasised by the fact that I do not remember meeting Louis Edwards until later in the season. I'm not sure that he even travelled to the Cup Semi-Final at Villa Park. He must have done, just as he must have been in the United boardroom after home games; but he did not push himself or make much effort to introduce himself to people until after Matt returned from Munich. Interestingly in this context, our paper's report of his co-option was taken from a news agency, and there was a quote from Mrs Edwards but not Louis himself.

Crisis management

The actual team, meanwhile, with whom I came to spend most of the time, was very insulated: on the road or at Blackpool as often as not. That was Jimmy's crisis plan, no doubt. Keep them close. Keep the inspiration and the concentration. Keep them away from the curious who wanted to talk, and the morbid who wanted to touch, and the press who wanted to rehash. Keep them in this group that had a holy mission. It is a classic psychological ploy, and David Meek and I were both subjected to it and willy-nilly became part of the support system. I knew more about football than David but he knew more about people, and meanwhile we had to try to be objective reporters on the men with whom we travelled, ate and lived in hotels, and who belonged for the most part to our own mid-twenties generation.

The pool of players that Jimmy used after Munich contained some who were very young and inexperienced: Alec Dawson, Shay Brennan, Mark Pearson, Bobby Harrop, Bobby English and the goalkeeper David Gaskell; first-teamers in Gregg, Foulkes, Charlton and eventually Dennis Viollet and Kenny Morgans; the imports Taylor and Crowther; and a group who had played in the first team but had been overtaken by more talented people – Greaves, Goodwin, Ron Cope and the Welsh international Colin Webster.

The balance of the team was good, and expressive of Jimmy's philosophy: even when it was being brushed aside it looked like Manchester United. A power fullback in Bill Foulkes was matched by the more ballplaying Ian Greaves. At right half Fred Goodwin was an excellent attacker in front of the rugged Foulkes, but he was slow to get back and Crowther was asked to play a more defensive role in front of the skilful Greaves. At centre half Ron Cope had quality but not enough steel: it was simply not in his nature. Up front there was great skill at inside forward, and speed along the flanks from Webster and Charlton.

Jimmy juggled his resources as much as he could, but there were always uncertainties in defence and the very young players became frazzled. Neither Alec Dawson, the centre forward for whom there were such high hopes, nor the dazzling inside left Mark Pearson, 'Pancho' for his sideburns and wicked tackling, ever truly recovered their careers.

The dilemma was that as games came thick and fast Jimmy dared not exhaust tired minds with detailed coaching. He had to inspire his key men for the big games and hope that with adrenaline their skill would deliver, which until the actual Cup Final it did, the attack scoring twelve goals in five Cup games.

But in the League there were a few draws, a couple of heavy defeats including one by Wolves, who won the Championship, some painfully narrow ones, and one victory, away to Sunderland, who were relegated.

The immortal

On the Saturday after the Sheffield Wednesday victory United played a solid home draw with Nottingham Forest, and had a week's grace until the sixth-round Cup tie at West Bromwich Albion. The young Bobby Charlton had returned from Munich and been sent home to Ashington, and one afternoon I went to the old Exchange Station in Manchester to meet him off the Newcastle train. 'We must get to him before the *Evening News*,' said Jack, and I was authorised to offer a weekly ghosted article at I think ten guineas a week. Bobby was a boy and no one on the platform seemed to know that it was him. The first article we did was about the players who had died, and he made pithy comments that were all the more affecting because he tried to be unemotional.

I had a correct but never very easy relationship with Bobby. I was an educated person whom he never entirely trusted, I suspect, because he did not know my agenda, and to me he has always seemed a tough nut, careful and contained. He has always said that life was 'paradise' in the days before the Babes burst upon the scene, when he lived in the club digs and shared innocent cinema-going pleasures; and he told me once about the first time he stayed in a hotel, with England Schoolboys, and did not know what all the knives and forks were for. But he would never look foolish or lose his dignity, and the hardness is a deliberate shield for the kid who knew paradise, I think, and for his romantic belief in football, which is why he was able to play so well. After the 1966 World Cup he talked to me about his fantastic goal against Mexico. 'I saw it on the replay,' he said, 'and I thought I'd been a bloody fool for shooting from that range.' But Jimmy Murphy and the pit-village kid within had given him the courage, hadn't they?

The kid was always in evidence, I thought, in his very observant sense of humour. He delighted in characters like Albert Scanlon, who because of his nose for gossip, and general sussing-out of hotel receptionists, cigarette machines, taxi ranks and nightclubs in hotel basements Bobby called the 'secret service'.

Later Bobby would visit us at home. He always liked my first wife, and she him. I am not surprised at what he has become – at his urbanity or the expensive hand-made suit he wore at the unveiling, or the way that as a United director he made sure that Johnny Doherty could not corner him. There were always depths to him, even when he was discussing American crooners with Dennis Viollet. On one occasion in the early 1960s I bumped into him in Kendal Milne's department store, and he talked about Ronnie Moran's coaching at Liverpool. This was long before the Boot Room became a legend, and if we ask ourselves the question 'Who first suggested that Manchester United should engage Alex Ferguson?' the answer is, I am sure, Bobby Charlton.

Droitwich

At the end of that week David and I went to Old Trafford
with our suitcases and boarded the team bus for the first
time. The coach was hired from Fingland's and the driver
was a lovely, lanky man named Ted, who always helped
Jack Crompton with the skip. There were a couple of
tables amidships but apart from that it was just a coach,
and there were twelve players plus Jimmy, Jack, David
and me, so the majority of the seats were empty. Most
of us lost money at three-card brag to Mark Pearson,
and the night before the match we stayed at the Raven
Hotel in Droitwich. It was dark and atmospheric and
had been furnished at the end of the 20s. It would have
been a good setting for an Agatha Christie story: the
drowning in his bath, perhaps, of a captain of Midlands
industry, with Poirot not impressed by the Brown Windsor
soup. I do not remember whether at hotel meals we
were on a fixed menu or allowed to choose. I think that
at match-day lunches we all ate the same, but that at
dinner there was some leeway for pressmen and officials.
Our great perk, of course, was that the club paid all our
travelling expenses, which David and I also claimed from
our papers. This was a considerable untaxed addition to
our salaries; and it was not until the 1970s that United
struck at David by withdrawing these facilities, since

when no reporters have been as close to the team as we were.

Although this was our first trip with the players we soon worked out who we leaned towards and who we didn't. Happily, David and I have always liked each other and it was not long before we formed a card school with Bill Foulkes and Jack Crompton. Busby had cracked down on gambling among the pre-Munich team but our game was hearts, very innocent and played for fun. The following season Albert Scanlon was an occasional member of the school, when his ludicrous attempts to fix the deal or the scores drove Bill to some memorable moments of fury. Once in a railway dining-car he rolled up the cutlery in the tablecloth and threw it out of the window.

I'm not sure why Jimmy Murphy took such a shine to me, but he did, and after dinner in Droitwich he asked me to sit up with him and ordered whisky, sugar and hot water. He was a man obsessed, a man whose life's work was in ruins, a man forced to re-evaluate. He needed to hear himself talk in order to work out what he thought about things, and I was the right kind of audience because in some respects I was very like him. Like him I was passionate about what I believed in. Like him I said what I thought, because arriving at what seemed true was the most important thing. Like him I had the romantic view that what was done properly would be rewarded, and that talent would be valued. Like him, and unlike Matt, I was no politician. I had a short fuse. Like Jimmy's, my feelings were on show, which never did me any good at all.

In the mythologising of Munich the fact that Jimmy

upset a lot of people has been glossed over. When he travelled from Munich with Harry Gregg and Bill Foulkes a crowd of reporters met the boat train and backed them against a luggage trolley.

'What's your next move?' someone shouted.

'My next move?' snarled Jimmy. 'My next move? I'm going to piss over you!'

There were mutterings among pressmen and in other boardrooms that he sent some of the players out to kick, and no doubt he did not discourage them. All in all, it was said, he was the perfect assistant, but not managerial material in his own right, and I agree with that. Of course, it did not stop offers being made, most notably by Arsenal at the end of the 1958 season, when the notion was that he would have taken Johnny Doherty as his assistant. He only refused, averred Johnny, because Mrs Murphy did not want to transplant their large and happy family to London. I think that it was more agonising than that, more a struggle of loyalties and self-examination, which made Jimmy happy to avoid the decision himself, and have Mrs Murphy make it.

At the time I believed as young people do (and some not so young) in secret histories and conspiracies, and Jimmy's revelations coloured my opinions. Matt gave three different newspaper accounts of how he took the signing-on papers to Duncan Edwards, said Jimmy, when actually it had been done by Bert Whalley. Matt was a bit of a villain, I thought, and Jimmy unrecognised and hard done by. Now older, I realise that the truth about them was both simpler and more unavoidably tragic.

Matt and Jimmy

Jimmy was a Catholic from the Welsh valleys, Matt a Catholic from the Scottish pit village Old Orbiston. Matt had lived with his parents and three sisters in a two-room cottage that had cold water outside but no sanitation. His maternal grandfather lived a few doors away, an amiable rogue of a kind that in later life Matt was always amused by, and often forgave. Matt was seven when his father was killed in the Great War, and ten when his mother re-married. There were two stepchildren. Matt was clever, and his schoolteachers wanted him to stay on until he was eighteen. But his mother and stepfather wanted to emigrate to America, and he did not. He left school and went down the pit so that he could pay his own way and anyone else's.

Written as a novel by someone of the time like D. H. Lawrence, this story would be about a boy wounded by the death of his father, seeking to replace him in his mother's eyes, and wounded again when she re-married. It would be about the way in which the boy's naturally outstanding bearing was enhanced by the need to mask his feelings in a cottage full of people striving amid poverty and drink to be respectable, and the risk he took in his acceptance of degrading labour. At the same time, in the novel by D. H. Lawrence, the boy

86

would have an unexpressed, yearning talent: he would be a poet or a painter, which is to say there would be a way of escape.

In Old Orbiston the way of escape was football, and the village had already produced three of Scotland's legends: Hughie Gallacher, Jimmy McMullen and Alex James, who was the finest inside forward of his time and became the playmaker for Herbert Chapman's Arsenal. Busby, the skip boy when James played for the village team, made steady progress in junior football. When his team Alpine Villa won the Scottish Under-18 Cup he was invited to join the prestigious Denny Hibs. Scottish junior football at that time was competitive and semi-professional, the forcing ground for a stream of good players; it is no wonder that having benefited from this, when Matt was a manager he took United's youth team to play in serious competitions in Zurich. Within two months of joining Denny, in February 1928, he was signed by Manchester City.

Murphy's early life was similar in outline but without the darker shadows. His home life in Pentre was poor but uneventful. He played the organ in his local church and football for Treorchy Juniors, from whom he was bought by West Bromwich Albion. Matt met his wife Jean, a Protestant, at a dance to celebrate Alpine Villa's cup win. Jimmy met his in Birmingham. On the field Matt was an artist. Jimmy was a hard-working wing half, nicknamed 'Tapper' for the ferocity of his tackles. Like most of the great football coaches he had to think about the game to make up for what he lacked in genius. Herbert Chapman was the same and so are Ferguson, Wenger, Mourinho and Benitez.

One of the matches in which Jimmy played for Wales,

then as now short of resources, was against France in Paris. France were assisted by the extraordinary coach Jimmy Hogan. According to what he told me, Jimmy wangled a romance with the great man's daughter in order to meet him and pick his brains.

In 1939 Jimmy was transferred to Swindon Town, but he never played for them because war intervened and he was called up into the Royal Artillery. He was sent to the Western Desert, and would speak with eloquence of those experiences and his memories of men weeping at the sight of the Mediterranean after months of sand. Years later he missed Munich because he was in Cardiff managing Wales in a World Cup play-off against Israel. The first leg had been in Tel Aviv.

'You'd have liked the hotel,' he used to say to me. 'It was smack on the Med.'

The Med had a poetic ring for him, and eventually he crossed it with the guns and landed in Italy. At some point in the campaign he was enlisted by Stanley Cullis, the captain and later manager of Wolves, who was a major in charge of an army recreational centre at Bari. Men went there for a week and were able to participate in all sorts of sports – better, it must have been deemed, than the dubious delights of Neapolitan brothels. Jimmy was a member of the football staff, and one of his duties was to give a weekly blackboard lecture on tactics.

Busby was a company sergeant major instructor in physical education. In 1940 he had taken a British army football team to play the French army in Paris, and early in 1945 he was told to assemble another team to play in liberated Italy. His second in command was Arthur Rowe, manager of Tottenham's push-and-run team in 1951, and the players included Joe Mercer,

Frank Swift, Tommy Lawton and Cliff Britten, the post-war manager of Everton. The order came at a vital time in his life. In December 1944 he had received the letter from Louis Rocca that hinted at the United manager-ship, and in February 1945 he went while on leave to meet James Gibson. He agreed to join the club on his demobilisation.

The army team left England in April 1945, just after VE Day, and toured Italy in their truck until June. One of their stops was at Major Cullis's recreation centre. Some accounts say that Jimmy was giving his weekly lecture in a field but he told me himself that it was in a Nissen hut. Wherever it was, Matt stood at the back to listen, and at the end invited Jimmy to join him at Old Trafford and coach.

So the most interesting question in the history of Manchester United is: what did Jimmy Murphy say in his lecture?

We always prefer to imagine that people who have achieved a great deal in their work together must like each other and be friends, but it does not follow. Stanislavski and Nemirovich-Danchenko, the founding geniuses of the Moscow Art Theatre, came to hate one another like poison. Considering how different they were beneath the simi-larities, Matt and Jimmy did not do so badly, even if the end was to be sad and distant.

Outwardly Matt was the calmer of the two, the less outrageous, the one who did not drink much or some-times sway towards women. Once in the crowded Old Trafford boardroom I saw him kneel to kiss the hand of the Bishop of Salford, but it was Jimmy, I think, who pondered his confession and had a rosary in his blazer pocket. Jimmy was a home and local pub person, the local being the Throstle's Nest in Whalley Range. Matt liked clubs and restaurants, theatres and the racecourse. He had some old friends like Len Langford, the former Manchester City goalkeeper, who had stood by him when they were young and Jean Busby had a succession of miscarriages, but the company of his famous years was racier.

They included the bookmaker Johnny Foy, Tommy Appleby, the manager of the Manchester Opera House, and Paddy McGrath, who had been a poor Catholic Irish boy in Collyhurst. A former boxer, Paddy stayed in Manchester during the war as a PT instructor at the RAF's Heaton Park embarkation centre and developed business interests in Blackpool. In 1954 he opened the Cromford Club, in the basement of a gloomy court among old office buildings. Later the site was built over by the Arndale Centre. There was a bar, a room for dining, dancing and cabaret, and a card room at the back. Paddy was a big, tall, dark, good-looking man, his style a northern reminiscence of nightclub owners in Chandler and Hollywood film noir: the inch of shirt at the cuff, the calmness, the cigarette tapped on the metal case. He was very kind to me and gave me an excellent piece of advice one night when I got drunk, went to the gents to be sick and arrived at the bar again.

'Keith,' he said, 'there's no shame in going home. The party's always there again tomorrow.'

Arthur Walmsley would have said that with its boxing weigh-ins, its big-race call-overs, its sporting hangers-on and its exaggerated respect for the ladies, the Cromford was not so much film noir as Damon Runyon. Arthur had a keen eye for the comedies of the local half-worlds, and one

The Dreamers: Jimmy Murphy (*left*) and Matt Busby

On the Maine Road terraces: United 6 Bournemouth 2, FA Cup 8/1/1949;
(*Above*) David Thirlby (*left*) and Keith Dewhurst;
(*Below*) Peter Thirlby (*left*) and Keith Dewhurst

Pictures snapped by David Thirlby at United trial match 1950/1:
(*Above*) Jack Rowley heads for goal; (*Below left*) Jimmy Delaney dives in the box;
(*Below right*) Keith Dewhurst outside Adney's Snack Bar, Colwyn Bay, *c.*1950

(*Above*) Old Trafford in the late 1950s; (*Below*) The *Evening Chronicle* sports staff:
(*left to right*) Keith Dewhurst, Jack Smith, Alf Clarke, Jimmy Breen (*obscured*),
Don Frame, Ted Coghill, Arthur Walmsley

(*Above*) David Meek with his trilby;
(*Below*) the old press corps in Nice:
(*left to right*) Frank Taylor, Henry Rose,
George Follows, Matt Busby,
Tom Jackson

(*Above*) The staff of the Rechts der Isar Hospital, Munich, visit Old Trafford, February 1958: (*extreme left*) Professor Georg Maurer, (*next to him*) the Lord Mayor of Manchester, Leslie Lever, Harold Hardman (*at microphone*), Bill Foulkes (*behind him to the right*); (*Below*) United Press Card, 1958/9 season

LEAGUE TEAM—continued

Date 1959	Opponents	Ground
Feb. 7	Tottenham Hotspur	Away
„ 14	Manchester City ....(5th)	Home
„ 21	Wolverhampton Wanderers	Home
„ 28	Arsenal ....(6th)	Away
Mar. 7	Everton	Home
„ 14	West Bromwich Albion ....(S.F.)	Away
„ 21	Leeds United	Home
„ 27	Portsmouth	Home
„ 28	Burnley	Away
„ 30	Portsmouth	Away
April 4	Bolton Wanderers	Home
„ 11	Luton Town	Away
„ 18	Birmingham City	Home
„ 25	Leicester City	Away
May 2	F. A. Cup Final.	

CENTRAL LEAGUE
FIXTURES

MANCHESTER UNITED F.C. CUP-FINALISTS 1958
Standing (*left to right*) : J. Crompton, Viollet, Scanlon, Goodwin, Cope, Gregg, Dawson, Crowther, Greaves, Harrop, W. Inglis.
Seated : Pearson, Brennan, Webster, Foulkes (Capt.) Charlton, Morgans, Taylor.
Inset : Matt Busby, Jimmy Murphy.

PHOTOGRAPH COPYRIGHT
OF MANCHESTER UNITED PLAYERS' COMMITTEE

Top) The Phoenix badge on United's Cup Final Shirt, 1958; (*Bottom*) the team photo postcard sold for the players' fund and taken to Italy by Fred Goodwin

After Munich. When you put on a red shirt: Jimmy Murphy harangues
Bobby Charlton (*left*) and Ernie Taylor at Blackpool

of his best stories was about what happened when the London gangster Jack Spot arrived in Manchester to impose his protection on illegal gambling. He had committed no crime, so the police got rid of him by having a word with the local gambling joint owners.

'Can we use steel?' asked the locals.

The police saw no reason why not, within the limits of discretion.

The locals went to see Spot in his room at the Midland Hotel. One of them had a meat cleaver under his overcoat, and Spot allowed himself to be escorted to the railway station.

There was a part of Jimmy Murphy that did not approve of nightclubs and Paddy McGrath, and when Paddy went to Old Trafford for free tickets, or on some obscure mission for one of the players or a family who had been bereaved in the crash, Jimmy would keep him waiting. Paddy would lounge against the wall of the old entrance, and chat to me and David as we came out with an air of sardonic comprehension.

Decades later I was given an ironic sidelight on all this when a neighbour in the Pyrenees was the actor and writer Scot Finch, whose aged mother I was amazed to recognise as having been the receptionist at Granada Television in the days when I spent many frustrated half-hours waiting for people to see me. Mrs Finch had been for many years the lady friend of Matt's buddy Tommy Appleby, and told me that socialising with Matt and Mrs Busby had never been easy because they disapproved of her unwedded state. There are pecking orders below pecking orders, after all.

Little Joe

When he started at Old Trafford Jimmy coached the first team, walking them through moves in the temporary gymnasium, and it took a while for the youth structure to be reassembled. Bert Whalley was made assistant coach after his playing career ended in 1948, and in 1950 Louis Rocca died and was replaced as chief scout by Joe Armstrong. Once again the title covered a multitude of politicking. Joe had worked for the Post Office and in his spare time been a scout for Manchester City, which is where Matt first knew him. Bert Whalley was a strong, simple Methodist, a northern chapel man through and through, and Joe was Catholic, a great provider of holy medals for the mothers of promising young stars, and when I knew him a small elderly man with a limp, a twinkle, crinkly grey hair and a fathomless gnome-like discretion. He had a tremendous fund of period dialogue, and used the same phrases to encourage or deflect.

'Hey up, Keith, lad!'

'Hello, Joe.'

'Heard the one about the two flies playing football in the saucer?'

'What?'

'One says to the other, "Hey up. Go easy. We're playing in the cup next week."'

With which he was gone, the reporter's question not even formed upon one's lips. He had an infallible way of delivering bad news, which was to begin 'Hey up, lad. You know how it is . . . !' and he and Jimmy had a collection of favourite anecdotes, which at appropriate moments they would take out of memory's cupboard and polish. Most were silly enough: a junior referee who went on without his pencil and could not book a player, or a youngster's mother who invited them to 'come and have a night out in Crewe some time'. And one concerned a Youth Cup game in which United had beaten Bexleyheath Youth Club 11–1. Bobby Charlton had scored with a piledriver that hit the stanchion at the back of the net and on its way out was caught by the goalkeeper, who thought that he had made a blinding save. Years later, in January 1989, I had dinner in an Italian restaurant in Hammersmith with the cast of a play written by Stewart Parker, one of my second wife's clients, who had died a month or two earlier. I sat near the leading lady's husband, a smallish man of ramshackle charm who directed TV commercials in Dublin. Someone had told him that I was interested in United and to engage me he said, 'As a matter of fact I played at Old Trafford.' It was him. The Bexleyheath goalkeeper. The figure of a comic football legend. I am afraid I was a coward and did not tell him.

One of the most powerful Murphy–Armstrong ploys, with Bert Whalley on hand to give the thing an air of rectitude, was to promise doubting parents or young players a meeting with the legendary Matt Busby. Bill Foulkes, for example, was earning what he called 'good money' in the coal mines and did not want to turn professional. He refused to meet Busby because he feared that if he did he would be charmed. In the end he succumbed and he was, but how much Busby knew beforehand about the person he had been wheeled in to hypnotise is a moot point and the essence of what Jimmy's conversation as we sat in cushy old armchairs in front of the lounge fire of the Raven was about. On the one hand, as Matt's assistant he had the best job in football. On the other he had a powerful sense of grievance and unfairness, on behalf of the dead Bert Whalley as well as himself.

The grievance

The extent to which Busby was or was not involved in the youth development work at United is a tangled subject, and the one to which late at night Jimmy Murphy always returned. Busby's charisma was a strange thing; for although most of the ideas that he expressed in ghosted articles or carried out in management were ahead of their time, what he said in conversation was bland and conventional. His secret was that you believed that he understood you and shared your dreams. His calmness seemed to have raised him above doubts. He embodied an ideal, and people wanted his approval. Yet if for some reason they got past that point, if they ceased to care about his approval, his magic no longer worked. It became obvious that what he thought was hidden, what he said unremarkable and what he did pure realpolitik: for the club, he said, in those desperate years in the 1970s when he made and broke four managers, but much of it was for himself, and the vanity and ambition that his manner made him seem not to possess. Jimmy Murphy knew this, and it hurt. He was after all the romantic above all others who wanted Matt to be a hero; he was the first person, in the Nissen hut in Bari, to have been offered the dream.

Busby's first newspaper life story, reprinted after Munich as a paperback, mentions Murphy, Whalley and Armstrong in generous terms. It also puts a subtle spin on things. Matt never said anywhere in so many words that Murphy was not just a talker about beautiful football, but the man who could make it happen. He never talked about Murphy's work with the first team, then or later. He never brought out the sheer drudgery and concentration of coaching. The amount of work put in by Murphy and Whalley, the energy and emotional drive that they produced several nights a week for an entire decade after working with the reserves in the day, can only be grasped when we put together the accounts of people like Charlton, Doherty and McGuinness.

Once, when Doherty had played a silly crossfield pass that gave away possession and a goal, Jimmy took him out alone and spent literally hours with him. Jimmy kicked the ball across the field; Johnny retrieved it. Jimmy explained why it was wrong, why you only give a crossfield ball when the play is condensed on your own side of the field. Then he kicked again, and Johnny retrieved again, and Jimmy explained again. If you do not find a spare man with a crossfield pass all that you are doing is playing the ball across the front of the opponents' defence without threatening them. Jimmy kicked. Johnny retrieved. Jimmy explained. A crossfield pass is not the same thing as the square ball, which you will often need to make at the beginning of a move to allow your own players to move ahead or around you. Then he kicked again and explained again from the beginning, and to this day you will see in a decent Manchester United team this understanding of the crossfield pass.

Or look at what he did with Bobby Charlton. He had Bobby Charlton repeat again and again his instruction 'Just hit the ball. Don't look up for the goal. Just hit it.' He would roll balls from different angles for Bobby to hit again and again, until the action became instinctive and turned him into the most spectacular sharpshooter of his day, the goal against Mexico being a classic instance.

And at the unveiling Wilf McGuinness reminded me of the day Jimmy sent him out to kick a ball against the Stretford End perimeter wall, bang it back and forth, first touch with alternate feet. Jim forgot that Wilf was there, and when he remembered, two hours later, Wilf was still at it. Jim said, 'Okay, son. Good. You'll do.' In criticism he could be abusive, but always with a kind word at the end.

The energy of this, the determination, the willingness to impose and reimpose one's personality in the pursuit of small faults and of making another person perfect, is extraordinary. It is the energy that was poured out, night after night, week after week, year after year; the energy that after Munich he never quite recovered; the energy that was barely acknowledged in public but was taken for granted and then forgotten in the myth that Matt allowed to grow around himself.

★   ★   ★

In Matt's defence, what I did not understand enough at the time was that much of his achievement lay in creating the conditions in which Jimmy and Bert Whalley could work. Since League football began in the 1880s the pursuit of short-term success had been as chronic as it is today, and although the big clubs had the potential to revive themselves no one achieved true eminence across generations of players until Herbert Chapman brought long-term planning and stability to Arsenal.

Like Chapman, Matt generated huge personal publicity. He showed the United board how their financial and youth policies needed time to develop, and insisted that there must be no interference. Could he have delivered the goods on the field without Jimmy Murphy? Probably not. Could Murphy have done what he did without the protection afforded by a Busby figure? Almost certainly not. Again, for Jimmy to manage Wales in short-term bursts was one thing; to have coached in detail as he did and at the same time undergone the day-to-day stresses of club management would have been quite another, and probably impossible for anyone.

The dilemmas

Such were the grief and emotions with which Murphy wrestled after Munich, when he did not even know whether Matt would live or be able to work again. He was like a musician having his scores destroyed, or a painter his canvases, while another artist got the rave reviews. I suppose that, having aspirations to be a writer, I understood this, and he perceived my understanding. The players, like the actors, are the public's heroes, but it is the manager who dreams.

Jimmy knew after Munich that everything would be different. 'We were set up here for ten years,' he said, but it could not happen again. For one thing, slush funds were pouring into youth football and United were ambivalent about them. Well before Munich, Busby's Coghill-written articles advocated the abolition of the maximum wage, freedom of contract and the reduction of the top two divisions to eighteen clubs each. The idea of the maximum wage was to give all the clubs an equal chance, but they never were equal, not even in 1887 when League football started. There were always clubs in larger-population areas who had more money, and from the outset they made illegal payments. It was a culture of hypocrisy which for years Busby refused to join. He ran United according to rules in which he did not believe, although he was aware that this gave him a moral hold over people. He arranged for cinema passes and similar privileges, but he would not pay backhanders.

A watershed was reached in 1957, when the Babes reached the Cup Final and the players were given a hundred tickets each, almost ten times the allowed limit. As an aside, no one has ever questioned how Duncan Edwards, a working-class boy of twenty-one on a basic wage of seventeen pounds a week, came when he died to leave ten thousand.

United did not like to be morally compromised, even when they knew they were, but youngsters had begun to expect inducements as a matter of course. They would never again be so easy to satisfy. Holy medals and respectable landladies would no longer be enough. Jimmy was almost fifty. Even if he could physically reproduce the energy he had possessed when he was forty, he did not have the heart to do so. But could he ever leave Matt Busby? Even though he could not create another team in the same way, could he ever leave United? Could he leave Matt and the club at this time of crisis, from which it would take God-knew-how-long to recover? Could he forsake their dream? How guilty would he feel if he did?

These were the real questions that swirled with the dissolving sugar in the whisky and hot water. On the other side of them is Matt Busby. How soon after he returned to England did he start to wonder the same things? When did he realise that he was stuck with a partner whose heart to do what he had been hired for was broken, but that it was upon this partner's football brain that the creation of another great team would almost certainly depend?

West Bromwich

West Bromwich Albion had beaten the full United team 4–3 earlier in the season and were many people's tip to win the Cup. They had a pleasing combination of power and skill, and their stars included Ronnie Allen, a scheming centre forward who lay deep, the inside forward Bobby Robson, who later managed England, and an excellent left half named Ray Barlow. Their manager Vic Buckingham told the papers that they would beat the makeshift United 6–0. This made us feel even more like men on a mission, and when the coach radio played 'The Ride of the Valkyries' it did not seem inappropriate. As we drew near the crowds grew dense. People drummed on the side of the coach. Inside the ground they roared and swayed. They spilled onto the pitch and back again, and celebrated football itself rather than one side or the other. United's explosive confidence gave them a two-goal lead but as they tired West Brom came back at them and at 2–2, in the dying minutes, Ian Greaves hooked the ball out of the yawning United goal. Decades later he admitted that the ball had been over the line, but nobody had protested because I don't think anyone wanted there to be a loser.

On the way home we stopped for an evening meal, and Jimmy was at Bobby Charlton all the time, encouraging and praising him.

'What did you think about him?' he asked me.

'He was brilliant,' I said.

'There you are. The press says you were brilliant.'

Bobby did not seem utterly convinced, but the replay was the game in which he implanted himself upon the national consciousness. It was a stalemate, the game in which Jimmy came down the tunnel yelling 'They're getting strung out!' In the last minute Ernie Taylor released Charlton, who went down the left in a great curving, heroic swoop, the defence outflanked, and his centre was so precise that Colin Webster tapped it in. Pandemonium. Desmond Hackett, the star *Express* man from London, was sitting on the press-box steps next to my seat with his portable typewriter on his knees, and did not look up in time.

'What happened?' he said.

I told him. His description next day was epic.

Two afternoons later Jack Smith and I were driven to Old Trafford by Bill Clarke, Alf's brother. We went out onto the pitch with Les Olive – promoted to United's secretary – and the chief inspector from Stretford police who had identified the bodies at Munich, and in what I would call the inside-right position of the team attacking the Stretford End, Bill scattered Alf's ashes.

On the drive back Bill said that the now-empty urn would make a handsome sports trophy, the only time I saw Jack Smith at a loss for a response. Next day United played West Bromwich in the League. Before the teams came out the tannoy relayed a crackling message: Busby's voice from his hospital bed. Then West Bromwich won 4–0. Since there had been no rain the white smear of Alf's ashes was still there, and players ran over and around it.

Semi-final

In the Cup Semi-Final United were drawn against Fulham, a Second-Division side whose principal player was the inside left Johnny Haynes. 'Eleven men,' said Jimmy in his team talk, 'with only one brain,' although another of them, the raking inside right Jimmy Hill, displayed brainpower of a different sort when he led the players' union to the abolition of the maximum wage. The view from the press box in the grand old Villa Park Stand, with its spaciousness and stained-glass windows the very temple of Edwardian golden-age football, was marvellous, and enhanced for me by the sight of Barry Cockcroft. Barry, later the maker of the outstanding TV documentaries about the Pennine farmer Hannah Hauxwell, was at that time a slyly amusing presence in our reporters' room. He was one of those people who always appear at events for which tickets or invitations are impossible to obtain, and there he was at Villa Park, strolling up and down the touchline. The match that he saw was an edgy 2–2 draw in which a tired-looking United were lucky to come out even.

Early home games after Munich were attended by the parents and families of the players who had died, and the club took a large invited party to Villa Park, with a stop for dinner on the way back. David and I sat with Bert Whalley's widow and brother-in-law, who when I ordered some wine said, 'I don't know how you can drink that stuff. Red ink!'

As the days went by more crash survivors themselves appeared. Jackie Blanchflower was unable to hide the depression that dogged him ever after. When he was a much older man he went through Belfast Airport and was asked, 'Was it you or your brother who was killed at Munich?'

'Me,' he replied.

Albert Scanlon, his flat cap above a ludicrous head bandage, and Dennis Viollet, in his Yves Montand rain-coat, also arrived, and travelled with the party to the replay at Highbury. The team's London hotel in those days was the Windsor in Lancaster Gate, a couple of Bayswater mansions turned into a warren of bedrooms and fire doors. It was grey misty weather in which the trees in the park were leafless ghosts. After dinner, Albert Scanlon took me and David to the Astor Club in Berkeley Square, an expedition heavily frowned on by the trainer Jack Crompton when he heard about it the next morning.

Footballers were among the first to wear the modish, tight-tailored Italian fashions of those days, and as well as his cap and bandage Albert had a short grey topcoat. We piled out of the taxi and as the doorman loomed Albert said, 'Albert Scanlon,' and we were shown at once to a strategic table. It wasn't that anything happened, that we drank outrageous drinks or made offers to the hostesses. It was enough to be there, in the gloom, and watch the waiters flick their torches on and off. One or two people came to shake Albert's hand, which he accepted as his due. He pronounced in his piping voice that it was the place where real toffs went; payment of our bill was waived; and we returned to the hotel.

Next morning we went for a walk in the park, up to the big statue of the horseman, and then piled into the bus to go to north London. It was the first day of the flat-racing season, and Alec Dawson asked me who would win the Lincoln.

'Babur,' I said. 'It's the uphill finish.'

There was a good mood on the bus, and it turned out that Jimmy had sat up all night and decided to replace the tired Mark Pearson with Shay Brennan. Charlton moved inside, which gave more thrust and inspired another burst of passion. There were bad moments in defence but going forward United displayed their quality, and won 5–3: Alec Dawson scored a hat-trick. Against all odds they had reached the Cup Final, which had been their ambition in the first place.

One of the ways in which the Arsenal stadium showed its premature modernity was the segregation of the press. They had their own tea room, away from the gossips of power, and David and I had to be out early to be sure that we did not delay the bus. It was waiting and we sat down. The players arrived, grinning.

'Well,' said Alec Dawson, 'you were right. Babur won.'

He had done it at 25–1 again, but this time none of us had backed him.

Jimmy winked and chuckled and said, 'All right, my old pal?'

'All right, Jim,' I said, and as the bus pulled away Dennis Viollet, who was in the seat in front of me, burst into the 'Busby Babes' calypso that they had recorded before the previous Cup Final. Other people added the chorus.

Then Dennis turned, Wembley in mind, and said, 'I think I'd better get fit.'

Busby's return

There were five weeks between the Semi-Final replay and Wembley. Meanwhile Bobby Charlton made his England debut, scoring the only goal against Scotland at Hampden Park, and we had two long away trips. Sunderland brought the one League victory. We stayed at Durham the night before, and the great amateur international Bob Hardisty came to the hotel to see Jimmy. There had been talk of him turning out for United after the crash, but nothing came of it, although the following season his Bishop Auckland colleague Warren Bradley, a schoolteacher who had moved to Manchester, became the team's regular right-winger. The other trip was to Portsmouth. We changed trains in London, where Jimmy had a comic confrontation with a drunk businessman who tried to sit in our reserved compartments.

He gave the second goalkeeper David Gaskell a game at Fratton Park and rang what other changes he could. Dennis Viollet got himself back, classy but frail after the accident, and emotional intensity began to fade into routine. Every week I ghosted for Bobby Charlton and wrote for the United programme. Both evening papers prepared Cup Final specials. Fred Goodwin assumed responsibility for the players' Cup Final fund and one of our photographers took the souvenir picture that they sold. Fred was tall, stooping and amusing and had had a spell as a fast bowler in county cricket. When the team bus passed shops or ads made familiar by television commercials Fred would as likely as not burst into the jingle. 'John Collier, John Collier, the window to watch!' His room-mate Ian Greaves giggled along with him. When we were away I would use their room phone if there was something wrong with my own, and as I dictated the team news they would lie in bed and mock my turns of phrase.

One day during the last week of April I was walking along under the Old Trafford stand when a cluster of people came out of the dressing room, and in the middle of them was Busby, like a sick emperor among his courtiers. He was haggard and used a stick, but as he greeted me by name and shook my hand he showed all the determination of power. All the people that I had seen every day for the past two months were behaving differently, I realised: Jimmy, Jack Crompton, Little Joe, Les Olive, Paddy McGrath at the great man's elbow. The time out of time, the time of miracles, had ended. Unfortunately, there was still the Cup Final to play.

Blackpool

We were at Blackpool for a week before the Cup Final, in increasingly warm and sunny weather. The days assumed a temporary routine: phoning stories twice a day, writing features, drinks with visitors from the national papers, walks on the hotel golf course to watch the training. Once they let me join in a kickabout, but I was disposed of before I could draw breath. Arthur Walmsley came over for a couple of days and the fun was excellent: he attracted various friends, one of them a businessman who borrowed my room for an hour to make love to his lady friend. Later she made an enormous pass at me, and Arthur advised me to get her over the next afternoon, which maybe I should have done, but I loved my wife-to-be and was idealistic, and did not think it right to behave differently from the players. Roy Paul, the great defensive wing half who anchored City's Revie plan, was famous for women in the team hotel, and Eric Todd's tales of them were among the most mind-boggling to be heard at the sports table. But United's discipline was strong. Talk there was aplenty, and on one memorable occasion the display of an unexpectedly erect member on the back seat of the bus, but there it ended. The action did not, as it were, take place at the office.

'They're fucking athletes!' Jimmy would declaim with a glare of certainty, and then realise from my expression what he had said.

Jimmy could affect a comic paranoia when he did not feel it, and would not go to the hotel bar because it was full of pressmen. So we would adjourn to pressman Arthur Walmsley's bedroom, and be off the record until the early hours. One morning after, I went to Arthur's room and could not believe the number of full ashtrays and silver-plated hot-water jugs. Arthur sat on the bed in his vest, scratched himself, read my mind and said, 'Oh, yes we did, my old pal!' Jimmy's greeting had by now become a catchphrase among the team and people close to me.

Conversation on these nights ranged from wartime experiences to Beethoven, Sibelius and the nature of soccer genius. The longer the evening lasted the less difference there seemed to be between, say, Beethoven's Funeral March from the *Eroica* and Tom Finney's left foot. Arthur had served in India, and his set-piece descriptions included child prostitutes at the gates of the camp, and men in the latrines afraid to look at their own urine in case it revealed blackwater fever. Jimmy evoked red-hot gun barrels, sandstorms and what he often said was as good a match as he had ever seen: it was in Bari, between a British team that included Finney, and Yugoslav former prisoners of war.

I have often wondered if Milorad Pavic was among the Yugoslavs.

Jimmy, as he more than once demonstrated when we happed upon a piano in some deserted hotel ballroom, was a great improviser in what one might call the manner of Rachmaninov, had Rachmaninov doodled rather than composed. David Sadler tells a story of being with United in a hotel in Portugal. The players rested in the afternoon but David was woken up by music. He followed it and found Jimmy in a huge room, playing to himself. The fact is that both he and Arthur had seen bad things in their time, were not sure that it was right to be detached, and believed absolutely that music offered consolation beyond words.

Words, meanwhile, were what we had for the here and now, and Jimmy particularly loved it when Arthur spun them around the Manchester boxing scene of the 1930s. There were three world champions, McAvoy, Brown and King, and Norman Hurst the Belle Vue promoter was also Kemsley's boxing correspondent. He allowed only one phone within reach of the ringside, and that was his own. As a youth Arthur had run copy for Hurst, and indeed for Douglas Jardine, the former England cricket captain, when Jardine wrote for the *Sunday Times*. He gave Arthur ten shillings, about the same as his weekly wage, for every day of a five-day Test Match. Another Arthur copy-boy story that made Jimmy chortle concerned a golf writer whose name I have forgotten. He covered the Open Championship at Birkdale, but to Arthur's consternation did not follow the players onto the links. It transpired that he already had the scoop of the day, having bribed a spectator to steal Henry Cotton's ball from a far-flung green.

When Jimmy talked about football it was our turn to be entranced, and he elaborated at Blackpool two of his most telling vignettes. They concerned Hughie Gallacher and Alec James, the legendary heroes from Matt's village Old Orbiston, and demonstrated the two faces of the place that in Matt, who was after all born a Gemini, somehow coexisted.

Gallacher was the short, tough ball-playing centre forward who led the Wembley Wizards' line when they destroyed England 5–1 in 1925. He eventually succumbed to alcoholic depression and threw himself under a train. At the time of the story he was just past his prime and at Chelsea. He went into the West Bromwich goalkeeper with his foot up, and Jimmy was one of the players who gathered round. The keeper's sock was rolled down to reveal a shin sliced open to the bone. 'There you are,' said Gallacher. 'You want to get a zip-fastener in that.'

The James story is inspirational, and the only people Jimmy talked about in similar terms were Law and Best. Jimmy was marking James in a game against Arsenal, and with his fullback had him hemmed against the touchline. James played the ball. They followed it and pounced – only to realise that what he had got them to chase was a flicked-up piece of mud. Wee Alec and the ball had gone the other way.

Jimmy's great pal among the pressmen had been George Follows, who died in the crash, and I think that those nights with Arthur were an attempt to recover some of the pure entertainment of friendship. They were not the soul-searching to which I had been witness on the road, nor the amused philosophising about the game to which we gravitated in the 1960s. They were wonderful nights, but unrepeatable, as though we were kids playing hookey.

★ ★ ★

In the last home game or two after Matt's return Louis Edwards had appeared in the Old Trafford boardroom, joshing but nervous, accompanied by his wife, who always seemed reserved in contrast to his crudeness, except that when we came to know him it was not so much crudeness as a complex assembly of brutal knowledge, vulnerability and eagerness to please. Their son Martin looked like his mother, tall against the bulk and the fat wet lips of Louis, and he was shy and watchful.

To travel hopefully

To meet the disliked enemy Bolton Wanderers at Wembley we went from Blackpool to Crewe, where we changed trains. We had to wait on the platform. People crowded round and a woman insisted on talking about the dead players, which upset Bill Foulkes. Eventually the London train arrived and we sat in a dining car in the afternoon heat. By the time we reached Euston energy had been sapped. The team bus drove past a John Collier window but there was no answering jingle. Since our last visits the weather had changed and so had the city. On Holland Park Avenue the leaves met overhead and the sun shone through them. There was blossom everywhere. The architecture gleamed white and opulent. We were no longer the knights come to do battle; we were uncomfortable provincials.

The hotel was at Oatlands, near Weybridge, where

Henry VIII had his palace on the river. It was pleasant enough and David and I played table tennis with Jack Crompton and Mark Pearson. On the morning of the game we went round the clock golf with Bill Foulkes. Then with Busby in his customary seat at the front the coach took us to Wembley, another hot and roundabout journey; Bolton, having got through their Semi-Final first, had booked the hotel nearest to the stadium.

Umbro, the kit manufacturer, at that time still a family firm in Manchester, had designed special shirt badges for both teams, and sent samples to be photographed by the paper. I still have them, in now-grotty passepartout frames. United's badge shows a phoenix arising from the flames, but it was not to be.

In the Wembley press box Arthur and I had seats a couple of phones away from Bill Clarke, who arrived in great high spirits in the Bolton coach. As they came up Wembley Way, he said, the players had sung two choruses of 'The Happy Wanderer', and were sure to win.

Having experienced the subdued atmosphere on United's coach and the effect of Matt's presence when half of his mind was not present at all, I feared that Bill was right. The game soon confirmed that he was. United's defence came out in an offside trap after a corner but Stan Crowther stayed where he was, and Bolton's centre forward Nat Lofthouse was in the clear, onside, and scored. United never got moving. They seemed weak compared to Bolton's power.

Jimmy must have done a tremendous focusing job at half-time, because they came out a different eleven. Fred Goodwin drove forward in the right half position and Viollet linked neatly with Charlton. The turning point almost came when Charlton burst clear on the left, but his shot bounced back off the inside of the far post. The ball was banged down to the other end, where as Harry Gregg turned to gather it, he was bundled into the net by Lofthouse for a goal that would never be allowed today and was dubious even then, although none of us reporting the match said so. The rest was anticlimax and playing out time.

At the end David and I went to the bottom of the stand and out on to the running track to walk round to the dressing rooms. There were a lot of other press there but Dennis Viollet ushered them out because Harry Gregg's ribs were bruised and he was groaning and yelling as the physiotherapist Ted Dalton strapped him up. David and I stayed and said, 'Don't worry. We'll be back next year,' almost our last act as morale-boosters. Matt looked drained, and Jimmy annoyed but un-surprised. There was champagne in paper cups. Then the bus, which was waiting in the tunnel under the terraces, drove us to Lancaster Gate, and later to the Savoy for the banquet.

Jack Smith was determined to get the pink to London and into the banquet before the *Evening News* green, and so we did. I gave the first copy to Sir Stanley Rous, the president of FIFA, who wasn't best pleased but put a statesmanlike face on things, and I distributed the rest around the River Room until my hands were dirty with newsprint. I left the banquet early, to meet my first wife and our friend the television director Herbert Wise.

The Sunday ride back on the train was bittersweet. The wives were with us, and some of the girlfriends of the dead. Eddie Colman's girl was a terrific bright spark who inked dots onto lumps of sugar so that we could play dice. At every station, even those at which the train

did not stop, there were crowds who waved and carried
United scarves and photos.

In the midweek there was a dinner at Stretford Town
Hall, where the clocks were to show different times on
the night of the unveiling, and then the bus took us on
a tour of Salford. To pass through the adoration of a crowd
is a strange experience, and I am not sure what it means,
any more than I am sure what it means, as David and I
did, to see our faces on posters one day and torn down
into the gutter the next. But a myth was kindled in those
days, and I shared the momentary invulnerability of its
heroes, when all of us in the team bus were young, except
for Jack Crompton and Jimmy, hunched in his overcoat
at the front, and outside there were the upturned faces
of people who wanted to dream. From the back-to-backs
of Salford, the heartland of Manchester United, whence
came Eddie Colman and Paul Scholes, we were carried
in that dusk after defeat to Manchester Town Hall and a
civic reception, whatever that actually is, in the big
neo-Gothic rooms decorated by Ford Madox Brown:
masterly frescoes which when they first saw them the
Victorian city fathers wanted to erase.

I never discussed it with Jimmy, nor even in all the
years after with David, but I have always thought that if
Matt had stayed away, if the prize had been to see him
at the end, to bring to the sick king the Holy Grail,
they might have held on to their invulnerability and
risen to the occasion of the Cup Final. They would
certainly have made a harder fight of it.

There remained, of course, when we unpacked our
suitcases, which after Blackpool and London were a
jumble of dirty clothes, the European Cup Semi-Final
against AC Milan.

PART FOUR
Milan

Schiaffino

I was used to English players by now and I had seen Real Madrid at close quarters on the field, but I had not stood next to the future of football until the AC Milan players came to Old Trafford for evening training. The light was dull and the stadium wet from earlier rain. Juan Schiaffino did not work out but watched in his street clothes. He had scored the vital goal for Uruguay in the 1950 World Cup Final pool, and was elegant with a movie-star smile and poise. The Swede Nils Liedholm jogged in a tracksuit. He spoke excellent English and asked me questions about the games after Munich. The composure of these men, lira millionaires and soldiers of fortune at ease in foreign lands, was something that of the United players I had met only Roger Byrne could begin to emulate.

United had to play both legs of the tie without Bobby Charlton, who had been claimed by England for their pre-World Cup touring party. They did well at home nonetheless, and won 2–1 on a cool and overcast evening. There was a niggle of dirty play throughout the match: the winning goal was a penalty, and Schiaffino went off for a time with a cut head. Liedholm was impressive as the midfield playmaker, and so was a blond Norwegian inside forward named Bredesen. Altogether the victory was a pleasurable surprise that gave a slightly false impression of what might happen in the second leg.

In those days European ties were big events followed by banquets, in Manchester's case at the Midland Hotel, with gilt-edged menus decorated with the club insignias. There had even been a banquet, at which Harold Hardman gave a moving speech, when Professor Maurer and his staff from the Rechts der Isar Hospital in Munich visited Old Trafford, and there was one now for the Milan party. A couple of days later we packed our bags again and went to London, en route to Italy.

Sometimes the club organised visits to the theatre but on this Saturday night they had not done so, and I went into the West End by myself to see a play by Jean Anouilh that starred Paul Scofield and Jill Bennett. She was a young girl with an extraordinary sexual presence, and made a great effect on me. Twenty-odd years later Scofield was in a play I wrote at the National Theatre, and the celebrity marriage of John Osborne and Jill Bennett was on its last vituperative legs. We would meet them at Bill Bryden's house. Time had been unkind to the once-magical girl, and made her spirit discordant.

Orient Express

Our journey from London to Milan was a giggle, more like a holiday than a serious assignment. In Paris, Les Olive, who carried a briefcase full of cash, asked me to walk with him down the platform as protection in the event of an attack. How international thieves were supposed to know about his burden I never asked. The train thereafter was the post-war version of the Orient Express, with the plates on the side that said SIMPLON-ORIENT, MILANO VENEZIA ISTANBUL, shorn of its glory but still glamorous to me, and the dining cars had dark art deco wood and frosted-glass decorations. David and I shared a two-berth compartment. We opened the doors to the next so that we could put a hassock in the middle and play cards. Jack Crompton did not win a hand the entire way from Manchester London Road to Milan Centrale.

Once in the early hours I lifted the blind and saw an Alpine mountainside. Then I drowsed again and awoke only when Italian passport control burst in with sunshine and glittering faux-naif smiles. 'Domodossola!' they cried, and peered curiously because they knew that we were Manchester United. Fred Goodwin, still running the players' fund, gave them team photos. The attendants brought coffee and buns. We washed standing up at the basin and got into our clothes, which we soon realised were too thick and northern for the weather.

Nowadays the route from the mountains to Milan seems to be all suburbs and industrial estates but then the plain was empty and crackled in the heat, and the outskirts of the city had the sudden raw ugliness that was to be immortalised by the classics of neo-realist cinema. Then the famous railway station dwarfed us, and we straggled out from its portals to see an awesome tower crane, which rose higher than the skyscraper Pirelli Building it was topping out.

'Will you look at that jig?!' yelled Harry Gregg, who had worked on building sites in his time.

Italian 1950s design

The bus took us to the Hotel Principe e Savoia, which had a belle époque facade and a redone marbled interior. The players were sent to lie down and the journalists walked out to look at the city. We were a mixture, because the number-one men from London were on the England tour and the Manchester dailies had not yet appointed permanent replacements for their men killed at Munich. The *Express* sent Henry Jones, a pear-shaped man with droopy eyelids whom Henry Rose had poached from the old *Daily Dispatch* because Jones came up with too many last-edition transfer scoops, which spoiled Rose's penchant for getting away early to his bridge club. I saw him there once, when I was taken by a friend from Granada Television who knew where an after-hours drink could be had: it was the first time I ate a smoked salmon sandwich. The *Guardian*'s man in Milan was Harold Mather, a gloomy, lantern-jawed rugby league writer who wore a tweedy suit and had underlying doubts about foreign food. I shared a room with him and he was astounded, a night or two later, by a Harry Gregg practical joke. Thinking that it was me and David in the room, Harry crashed open the door around midnight and pelted us with shoes that had been left out for cleaning.

'It's still a bit bloody strange,' said Harold, 'even if it was you and Meekie.'

We journalists pretended, as we returned from that first stroll, that we were dazed by the heat and our tiredness, but it was more than that. It was more, even, than Italy's age-old ability to absorb and stupefy invaders from the north. It was the energy and style of Milan itself that knocked us sideways, a city at a dynamic moment in its history.

Today every schoolgirl who reads a fashion magazine has some notion of Milan, although the clothes are in a sense the decadent phase of a great period, the last energy of a city that is polluted, overcrowded and in places dangerous. When I subsequently went there in 1981 with our friend the furniture designer Peter Wigglesworth we toured the clothes shops not to see the clothes themselves so much as the ways in which the shops had been designed, in variation after variation of a modernism that had not yet appeared in London, the single exception being the shop which Peter himself designed for Paul Smith in Floral Street, Covent Garden.

In 1958, however, Milan's creativity was at its height. Gio Ponti, the architect of the Pirelli Building, was ageing but alive, and most of the other great names of architecture and design, the men who shaped so much of what we call the style of our time, were at the top of their powers: Vico Magistretti, Joe Colombo, Marco Zanuso, Castiglioni. The companies that made and marketed their work were young and vital: Zanotta, Danese, De Padova, Oluce. The Milanese films of Luchino Visconti and Antonioni were still to come, but Giorgio Strehler was at the Piccolo Theatre, and at La Scala Visconti had directed

Maria Callas in five operas, of which the conductors were Serafin and Giulini. And 1958 was the year in which the Milanese house of Feltrinelli published Giuseppe di Lampedusa's great novel *The Leopard*.

Of these activities we were provincially unaware, yet their energy and atmosphere, the way the city looked and its people behaved, overwhelmed us. They made us insecure. I was in a daze all the time that I was there. I knew that I was in the presence of something wonderful, but not what it was.

Booking a telephone

Before I left Manchester the office cashiers gave me a wad of traveller's cheques to pay for the hire of a phone in the San Siro press box. We arrived in Milan on Monday morning, and that afternoon I went to the Italian telephone offices to make my arrangements. A charming young man in shirtsleeves explained to me that the previous week a championship boxing match in Milan had been cancelled. The *Daily Mirror* had paid for a ringside phone that was never put to use, but the young man realised that the football was in the offing and had maintained the reservation.

'Are you from the *Daily Mirror*?' he said.

'No.'

'It is of no importance,' he said. 'You can use the phone for a much smaller sum.'

This was my introduction to an aspect of Italian life to which, when for a time in the 1970s I owned a house in Tuscany, I became ruefully accustomed. In short, money changed hands, and with what was left over I bought at the end of the week a light grey mohair suit from a shop in the Galleria Vittorio Emanuele, and had them shorten the trousers. The players were impressed, Bill Foulkes in particular.

Red shoes

In an official biography of Matt Busby written by Rick Glanvill in the mid-70s and recently republished in a revised form by United themselves, Matt describes how after the crash he blamed himself for not stopping the fatal air journey after two attempted take-offs had failed, and how he felt guilty because he survived when others did not. This is a well-known phenomenon and one that I experienced myself when I was hit by a car at a time when two of my friends, the actor Brian Glover and the TV producer Geraint Morris, were dying of incurable ailments. My irrational question was: why had I escaped so lightly? Imagine how much worse this was for Busby, who had been among his people when they were killed, and was a Catholic who had always believed in a merciful God and an afterlife. In the Glanvill book he says that after Munich his faith was shaken, and I believe him. I think that the sorrows and doubts of that event haunted him for the rest of his life; and when he adds that for a time he never again wanted to have anything to do with football, that he could not face the Wembley dressing room after the Cup Final (although I saw him there as plain as day) and that he avoided the Milan games altogether, I think that he is wrestling with a dark angel he could never quite defeat.

He tells the author–interviewer how a despairing man spent six weeks in a Swiss resort, where he was healed and found reasons to go on: for the lads and the club and the beautiful game, and the winning of the European Cup that would lay the troubled spirits to rest. Except that he is speaking years after the cup was won, and the only need for a justification was his own. What haunted him was that he had continued with the flight because to arrive in England too late for the Saturday game would have incurred a fine and the loss of points; and the opponents were Wolves. To arrive only just in time would have meant jaded players in the season's most vital game.

He wrestled for years, I am sure, with the thought that these considerations were the price of the other side of his nature, the side that actually won the European Cup in 1968, the one that was ruthless in its will to conquer his ailments and reimpose himself. And the two sides were interlocked. He exhausted himself at the FA Cup Final, I think, and he was in despair and he did find solace in Interlaken, where he went with his wife and Mr and Mrs Louis Edwards, in Louis's grey Rolls-Royce, calling in at Milan for a day or two, where I had numerous earnest conversations with Mrs Edwards about a pair of red high-heeled shoes that I had seen and eventually bought for my wife-to-be. Mrs Edwards had noted the shop and had a good idea of how continental sizes translated into English. I liked her a lot. She was very correct. I have always thought that she was lonely but too proud to let it show.

They had driven to the Continent from the Cup Final. I'm not sure that they did stay for the game, but they were around for a while, and I remember the big Rolls on the hotel concourse one afternoon when we bumped into two Englishmen who had turned up in the hope of meeting a player or two: bizarrely, they were Bill Sowerbutts and Fred Loads from the BBC's radio show *Gardeners' Question Time*.

That may have been when Fred Goodwin and I returned from meeting a businessman to whom Fred had been recommended in the hope of arranging for the players' fund team photos to be sold to the crowd outside the stadium. A fool's errand if ever there was one. The Milan supporters were more likely to have burned the seller along with his photos than to have parted with a single lira. It was another eye-opener to see the man, however, as he conducted his import-export business over two or three phones at once, and in as many languages. He gave us coffee and treated us as though we were important but idiots. I think that in the end Fred gave the photos to waiters in lieu of tips.

It was still sunny on the evening we went to watch the training, at an old stadium near the city centre. Various unexplained Italians turned up, one of whom hit me on the back of the head with an attempt to return a ball from the sidelines. We had a travel courier with us here, and indeed every time the bus turned up.

He was a thin, faded, ex-military type of Brit in a worn blazer who thought that because we were young we would like dirty jokes, but we didn't really, or at least not from him.

Defeat

The game kicked off late, maybe even at nine, and it was dark when we arrived at the San Siro, which blew our minds again, first by the spirals of lights that rose with the external access ramps, and then by the two tiers, the din, the flares and the animosity. A few minutes after the kick-off the referee blew for a minute's silence for someone who had died, an event whose timing bewilders me to this day, and once when a United player committed a foul I was punched by an Italian in the row behind. There was a loudspeaker in the tiered concrete immediately above the press box and dictating was a nightmare of reverberations. It made me laugh out loud. Brian Glanville, then as so often the best British press judge of foreign football, told me later that he had read in *La Gazetta dello Sport* a description of a fair-haired English journalist who was *simpatico* because he laughed at the absurdities, and knew at once that it was me.

What happened in the game, alas, was no laughing matter at all. Milan had played tricks with the squad system in the first leg and appeared now with venomous attackers. Liedholm and Schiaffino did their stuff; shirts were tugged, bodies checked, the referee intimidated, ankles hacked and retaliation met with outrage and overacting. The outside left Cucchiaroni, whose name Bill Foulkes pronounced as 'Caterpillar', was outstanding both as a player and a cheat, and it was he who Bill deposited against the fence. At the other end Alec Dawson was grabbed round the neck, flung to the ground, and had a free kick given against him. Ernie Taylor had his moments, which the crowd applauded, and Harry Gregg looked every inch the mad Irishman, at which they jeered. Milan's 4–0 victory was an accurate reflection of what occurred. But it rankled. The sheer insolence of the gamesmanship made us feel stupid. And of course some of Milan's football did glitter.

When the game ended the tannoy blared music and I hollered off-the-cuff material into my phone for a quarter of an hour, watched by spectators who must have gathered every week to watch journalists make fools of themselves. The charming young man who had hired me the phone was there, and shook us all by the hand. From his point of view it was a job well done. Then I walked down the ramp with two elderly foreign journalists.

'The masters and the pupils,' one of them said to me.

'Unfortunately,' I said.

The man turned to his colleague and said, '*Madrid va gagner.*'

They knew that I had to find the United dressing room to link up with the bus and took me under the stand. I passed the Milan room, which was bare and cavernous and full of animated talkers, and shook hands with Liedholm. He was in his raincoat. I congratulated him and he grimaced and said, 'Safe journey.' Whether he meant the Orient Express or the team bus I am not sure, because there was a police guard and a bit of shoving and abuse.

Over twenty-four hours the hot weather had become grey and sultry and after the game it broke. Thunder growled and there was rain. When the teams lined up before the kick-off the United players had each been presented with a cardboard-boxed Milan cake, which seems to me now an agreeable kind of preserved confectionery, delicious when heated up and served with, say, mascarpone. To our aggrieved and body-checked soldiers it seemed like insulting foreign muck. I am not sure how, in the early hours of the morning, I found myself on the hotel's roof terrace, but I did, and as we looked down on the wet concourse, the smart cars and the staff in their fawn uniforms and white gloves one of the reserve players unwrapped his cake and dropped it like a bomb upon the sophistication below. Others followed suit. I have been in a good few drunken imbroglios at the National Theatre and related late-night restaurants, but this bombardment from the roof of the Principe e Savoia is the only time I have been involved in a rock-and-roll-style incident. Oddly enough nobody complained.

The post-match banquet was held the following evening, in a suite of private rooms at Savoni, the great restaurant in the Galleria. Bredesen, the Norwegian who had played at Old Trafford, sat at a table adjacent to mine. One of the Italian officials made a speech about sportsmanship, at the towering summit of which Bredesen grinned at me and rolled his eyes. Then we were given enamelled AC Milan lapel badges. I still have mine, in my stud box, although I have never worn it.

The hotel at Stresa

On the day after the match we were taken on a coach trip to Stresa. The weather was poor, but even in drizzle the scenery of the lakes is magical. We stopped outside the front of the Grand Hotel des Iles Borromées and walked through the imposing central entrance. I was with David and Jack Crompton, and as soon as we were inside the belle époque splendours I had a sensation of having been there before, which plainly I had not.

'If we go down those stairs,' I said, 'there's a billiard room.'

We went down and there was.

Amazement.

Months later I realised that this is the hotel in Hemingway's novel *A Farewell to Arms* in which the semi-autobiographical hero plays billiards with the old count, and that by some trick of the mind the description had come back to me.

After lunch we braved the rain and went in the hotel's motorboats to Isola Bella, the fabled baroque palace built on one of the lake's little islands. One of the staterooms was picked out in silver, and outside the windows there was grey mist and flat grey water.

Stresa and the Italian Lakes caught my imagination that day, and although I have never spent as much time there as I would like, my second wife and I were lucky enough once to be lent a villa in a hill village above Lake Lugano, and we did stay a few times in the hotel at Stresa. The last time I was there was in November 1995, when I broke a train journey for a sentimental night's return. The town was empty and the island palace closed for the season. There were many signs of mass tourism and heavy lorries boomed along the widened main road from time to time. I was the only person in the hotel's lounge bar, with the huge windows that overlook the lake, although there had been a business conference earlier in the day. I don't drink any more and ordered a tomato juice. It came on a silver tray with a napkin and an array of cocktail snacks. The barman wore a white jacket with gold braid. He inclined his head and asked a formal question or two about my journey. It was perfect and about a hundred years out of date, but we both felt good about it, and I for one knew that Hemingway would have approved.

The banquet was on the evening of our visit to Stresa, and the next morning, our last, Jimmy Murphy asked me to go with him to see Leonardo da Vinci's *Last Supper*. Jimmy had kept himself to himself a lot in Milan. I think he knew that as a football mission it was doomed, and in his head he had already moved on to the next: the management of Wales in the impending World Cup Finals in Sweden.

PART FIVE
The World Cup 1958

Dundonnell

A news desk's paranoia about its men in the field is endemic, and our otherwise relaxed sports table was not exempt. They would put me in a hotel, book a call not just to the building but to the room, and when I answered yell 'Where are you?' in panicked tones. It was a joke between us that had more meaning when, at the end of the week of my return to Manchester, I took my accumulated days off as a holiday. I had a Cambridge friend who was doing research at St Andrews, and so we flew to Edinburgh and took a train. After a couple of days we hired a car and drove into the Highlands. 'Wherever you are,' Jack Smith had said, 'keep in touch.' We were at Dundonnell, hundreds of miles north, where the mountains tumble down to Little Loch Broom, when we stopped for coffee at an inn and I amassed enough small change to make a call.

'Where are you?' shouted Don Frame, his voice far away, as voices were on the phones of those days. When I told him he groaned.

'Turn round!' he cried. 'Arthur's ill. You've got to do the World Cup in Sweden.'

That was Tuesday. We caught the last Wednesday flight from Edinburgh and on Friday I went to Hull, to sail to Gothenburg on the weekly cargo liner *Cicero*. There were three other passengers, two of them lady publicans on a cruise. At mealtimes the captain made great play of the fact that his regular cargo was British parts for what he called 'that hundred-per-cent-Swedish car the Volvo', and aired his cynicism about Sweden's wartime neutrality and the money they had made from trade with Germany.

Planning

It was legendary in Manchester journalism that the executives of the *Daily Express*, then a super-efficient organisation, always worried about the resources that Kemsley might throw into the field against them: extra men, vans with mobile stop-press machines, relays of cars to carry picture plates. It was equally legendary that, however much the *Express* men worried, and whatever counter-plans they devised, Kemsley never organised a thing in the first place, because like many inefficient organisations they worried all the time about costs.

This is why I was sent to Sweden by train and boat rather than air. Stars went by air, and the *Evening Chronicle*'s men did not come into that category. Paradoxically this gave me an enormous advantage, because I was the first English reporter from any paper to arrive in Gothenburg, and had written five or six background pieces before anyone else had started. To sail up the rocky-shored and many-islanded Gothenburg estuary was a splendid way to arrive, and although my hotel booking did not start until Monday, I went ashore when we docked on Sunday evening to check it out. The hotel was luxurious and little had changed since the 1920s: there was the dark-wooded comfort of the north, and in the dining room songbirds in elaborate cages.

Needless to say, however, in true Kemsley style there was no record of my booking, but I did have my side of the documentation, and when I returned next day they gave me a poky little room over the front entrance. I was to pay for the room and all my food at the hotel with coupons which newspapers had to buy from the World Cup Organising Committee, and I soon realised that if I bought a drink or a packet of cigarettes with a coupon I received a lot of cash in change.

Phones were considered too expensive, and there would be no 'Where are you?' except in dire emergencies. I had a cable card to use at the Ullevi Stadium or the Western Union offices, and it was when I went to confirm all this at the stadium, and to get my photo stuck into my press card, that I met Nick Hjorth.

Nick was about forty and resembled a tall but still shambolic Groucho Marx. His wife was on an island somewhere, as Swedish wives would be at that time of the year, which gave him full scope to carry out his press liaison duties. He had Olympic medals for yachting, about which he wrote for the local morning paper, and we took a liking to each other. When I said that I hoped my wife would come over he suggested that I cash in my hotel coupons and move into his flat, which after a day or two I did.

Brazil

Hundas was a ski resort thirty miles from Gothenburg and two of England's Group Four opponents, Russia and Brazil, had moved into the hotels there. The Russians were nearer the station and I wandered into their lobby at the very moment that their political officer Dimitri Posnikov, who wore a richly embroidered peasant shirt, was giving team badges to the hotel staff. He pinned one to my lapel before I could explain who I was, and when I did he said that he had thought I was the assistant manager.

Towards lunchtime I strolled the 200 yards through the forest to the Brazilian hotel, from which samba music blared all the time. I enquired at reception for the team management and could not understand why I was kept waiting. When the charming Brazilian official Hilton Gosling and the coach Vicente Feola at last appeared they laughed. One of the receptionists had spotted the badge in my lapel and assumed I was Russian. The two teams had been living within music-shot of each other for at least a week, but there had been no official contact, and my arrival caused a diplomatic flutter.

Feola was short, plump, battle-scarred and amusingly frank. He said that England's chances had been wiped

out by the Munich disaster and that Russia were over-
rated. His own task, he said, was to make the Brazilians
play as a team, which he did not believe they had ever
done in what he called 'serious international competition'. Stars who would not cooperate with him had been
left at home, and there were only four survivors from
the 1954 World Cup squad.

His openness was as marked a contrast to the bland-
ness of the Russian coach Antiponek as the riotous
samba style of his players was to the disciplined polite-
ness of the Soviets. After I had talked to Feola I ordered
a salad and a lager, and watched a group of his players
kicking about for fun on the hotel lawn. They flipped
the ball from one to the other in a circle, and it hit
the ground about twice during the time it took me
to eat. As I was leaving, the little outside left Zagallo,
later their manager in both triumphs and disaster, came
down to post a letter. He smiled at me and shook my
hand.

The following evening I took the train to Boras to
watch the Brazilians in a practice match against a local
team. It was played at a beautiful little ground
surrounded by trees, and, in the long, evening light of
the northern summer, which lingers until in the early
hours a greenish tinge heralds the dawn, Brazil gave all
their players a run-out except Pelé. There were bewil-
dering positional switches but a pretty rigid adherence
to the 4–2–4 formation, and in my cable I picked out
Didi, Garrincha and Mazzola.

At such events there are always spies and rumours,
and the Austrian coach Josef Agauer, whose team com-
pleted the group, gave an impromptu spin-doctoring press
conference at which he said, 'You can hide many things

but you cannot hide bad finishing.' Which is to say that the Brazilians could have scored twenty-five but in fact got four. What struck me was the rigidity of their back four. It was as though in their determination to meet Feola's ideal of teamwork, they held their shape when they should have responded to a crisis – which meant, I thought, that they could be penetrated by a well-timed thrust. Nevertheless, my cable's conclusion was that on the day, if Brazil's shooting matched their approach play, they would master the world.

England

English journalists started to arrive on Thursday, and on Friday evening we all went to the swish, modern Park Avenue Hotel to welcome the team itself. They were the last party to arrive in Sweden. Foreign journalists were amazed by this, and by their choice of a big-city hotel. The manager Walter Winterbottom said that they had been happy to stay and train at Roehampton, and that anyway his players were city boys. Winterbottom was a very decent man and came from that cotton-town background, in his case Oldham, of a respectable working class that sought to better itself through grammar school education. He had been an amateur with Manchester United, and in the war won that badge of middle-classness, a commission. He was highly qualified in physical training and a good organiser, and the FA made him their first team manager and head of coaching in 1945. He was tall, with wavy hair and a pleasant but serious demeanour. He did not pick the England team, of course: that was done by the International Selection Committee, which he attended in an advisory capacity.

As the players waited for their room allocations Bobby Charlton and I made a beeline for each other, I introduced myself to Tom Finney, and Winterbottom disarmed the foreign press with his airy charm. He had a boyish grin, smoked a pipe and was as honest as the day is long. As I watched him I thought about the famous practice match at the Cliff when England played United Reserves and were beaten 6–1. Johnny Doherty was United's deep-lying centre forward, and as Jimmy said, 'It started out like a practice but they were spitting chips at the end.'

Some time later more or less the same United side played Chesterfield Reserves, the lowest of the low, and Bert Whalley refused to give a team talk because 'as you know, there's enough talent in this team to beat England'. Chesterfield won 2–1: Bobby Charlton's grin at the memory was always infectious.

Next day a good-sized crowd watched England train at the Ullevi. Winterbottom was pestered again by foreign journalists, who wanted to know why he had selected the big, clumsy West Bromwich striker Derek Kevan. English pressmen watched and waited. They suspected that the question was a good one, because the point about West Brom was that the schemers, centre forward Allen and wing-half Barlow, were not in the party. Even West Brom's Bobby Robson, who was expected to play for England, was not their real provider; and if England wanted a battering ram there were better ones than Kevan left at home.

'Why has everyone got Kevan on the brain?' Winterbottom smiled as though it was part of some organic process and not an expedient enforced by Tommy Taylor's death at Munich. It is a measure of Winterbottom that I do not recall him saying at any of his press conferences that the loss of Byrne, Edwards and Taylor had robbed the team of a spine as well as three great players. It was naive of him but it was brave, and he was a mixture of the two.

Within a couple of weeks, of course, the Selection Committee's decisions came back like ghosts to haunt them.

Baltic schooner

On Sunday, the morning of England's first match, the weather turned grey and wet and Nick Hjorth took me sailing. We were on one of the judge's boats for a race where the river met the sea, and spent an uncomfortable time yawing up and down as smaller yachts tacked around us. But there was one marvellous moment, when out of a squall scudded an old-time Baltic schooner, leaning under full sail, and still trading after a half century or more. Nick's car was at the dock, and when we come ashore we threw our oiled jackets into the boot and went to the Ullevi to see England play Russia.

It was one of those half-disasters familiar to England fans. The Russians man-marked Winterbottom's play-maker Johnny Haynes out of the game and went two up. England struggled back. Kevan scored with a header from a long ball forward, and the Russians committed many fouls. Finney was hurt but still brilliant: it was through him that England kept in the game. With four minutes to go Haynes was tripped and Finney hobbled up to score from the penalty spot.

At his press conference Antiponek remembered me and said with a wink, 'Haynes threw himself into the penalty area. Very foxy.' The press room contained typewriters in different alphabets and a Brazilian rushed in, touch-typed his story, and ran into the cable room, where he realised that what he had was a mess of Cyrillic characters.

Next morning my wife arrived on the passenger ferry from Harwich.

Finney's knee

At the Park Avenue Hotel and the England training sessions in the old wooden Ullevi it became obvious that the story was the injury to Finney's knee. Would it keep him out of the game against Brazil? It did, and Alan A'Court of Liverpool took his place in a match that stays in the mind as a defining moment. This is an odd thing to say about a o–o draw that never exploded into passion, but what it demonstrated was that Feola's teamwork was there to stay, and that although the team produced by England's soccer culture had the where-withal to hold the Brazilians, it did not have the skill to overcome them.

There were two key periods in the match. At the end of the first half the Brazilian inside right Didi got away from his marker Bill Slater and tortured the England defence, but Billy Wright held firm at centre half, and the Burnley goalkeeper McDonald, a great player whose career was wrecked by injury, made some splendid saves. Then at the end of the second half, when Brazil had run out of ideas, England came forward: they were first to the ball in midfield and the Brazilian defence was stretched and rocking. But England did not have the skill to sweep through them. Maybe Finney would have provided it, or the boy Charlton, who was left on the bench. Who knows?

In the other group match that evening Russia beat Austria. So Brazil had three points, Russia three, England two and Austria none. Expectations alter with events, and in my next cable I said that England *must* beat Austria because Russia's tackling and quick passing could get them a result against Brazil: a view of the eventual champions that history, being written by the winners, has denied. Yet I saw what I saw. Brazil had been there for the taking in the last quarter of that 0–0 draw, and there were players left behind in England who were good enough to have got through a back four that was good individually but awkward as a unit. Sometimes, where history is concerned, the memory of the losers is more accurate than what is afterwards said in legend.

My wife and I were very happy during those weeks in Sweden, perhaps as happy and fortunate as we ever were together: young, in the summer in an agreeable city that had not known wars, with interesting events to attend and write about, and that lack of responsibility for them that is the true journalistic adrenaline. We had dinners at the Press Club, strolls in the white nights, amusing people to chat to, like Brian Glanville and Geoffrey Green, the marvellous louche old sophisticate who wrote on soccer for *The Times*, and a flat to be private. We were sure that life would go on in such a way, and that I would have the luck and success in writing that I had enjoyed on the paper. No wonder, perhaps, that one is drawn to the might-have-been.

Smack on the Baltic

Jimmy Murphy, meanwhile, had been soldiering on as manager of the Welsh team in a group with Sweden, Hungary and Mexico. He had sole responsibility for team selection and an able confederate in his captain, the Arsenal wing half Dave Bowen. They were staying at Saltsjöbaden, an old bathing resort outside Stockholm, and I had phoned him before each of his matches.

'Come over,' he said. 'You'll like the hotel. It's smack on the Baltic.'

Indeed it was: its belle époque splendours rose a few yards from the rocky, wooded foreshore, and it was along its corridors, beneath its chandeliers and ormolu clocks and glimpses of ourselves in watery mirrors, that Jimmy and my wife and I played hide-and-seek with Bernard Joy of the *Evening Standard*, Arsenal's emissary in their attempt to hire Jimmy as manager. Bernard had been on our train from Gothenburg, but we were first to the hotel, where we discovered that Jimmy did not want to talk to him. So we were dragged around corners, and from room to room, when Bernard's imposing figure strolled into view. He was a tall and charming man with a diffident sort of authority, who as an amateur had been Arsenal's first-choice centre half. At the time I thought that he had come to *make* the offer to Jimmy, but I am sure now that he had come for an answer, which Jimmy did not have. Then on one of our escapes into the hotel grounds we saw an angular, elderly little man getting out of a taxi with a touch of arthritic difficulty.

'See that man?' said Jimmy. 'Do you know who it is?'

We didn't, but it was Alec Morton, one of the Scots Wembley Wizards who had beaten England 5–1 in 1928.

The match in Stockholm that night was between Sweden and Hungary. I was able to get into the press box and Jimmy gave my wife a VIP ticket from the Welsh FA, so at half-time she found herself taking tea with the Swedish royal family. Half of Hungary's stars had defected to the West in 1956 and Sweden were deserved 2–1 winners, although the Hungarian goal was a spectacular rocket from Tichy. This was the only time I saw the Swedish veteran Gunnar Gren, back home after a decade in Italy. He had lost pace, but one could see from what he tried to do, his changes of balance and incisive thrusts, how exciting he must have been at the 1948 Olympics.

In the sleeping car on the way back we did not wake up in time, and harassed officials dragged us out. We went back to the flat to shower and on to the Old Ullevi to watch the British press play the Swedish. Bernard Joy was at centre half and I can still hear him shouting to his forwards, 'Come back, Lorenzo! Come back!' Lorenzo being Peter, father of the sometime TV sports anchorman Matthew. The Swedes won, I think, despite the barracking of real England players like Billy Wright.

Later in the week we hired a taxi for a day and went to see the Irish in their training camp at Tylösand, a little bathing resort amid sand dunes. We had an amusing sandwich lunch with the manager Peter Doherty and his captain Danny Blanchflower, surely the best talker of a game there has ever been. He quizzed me in detail about the different national training routines that I had seen. Meeting Doherty was for me more an event of hero worship. Even as a veteran he was one of the best forwards of my teenage years, a truly heroic presence as season after season he saved Huddersfield Town from relegation. Before the war he had played for Manchester City: in their dazzling Championship team of 1937 and the following season in the side that scored more than a hundred goals and still managed to be relegated. I asked him about it but he had no explanation. Even Danny was at a loss for once.

Knocked out

England's last group match, against Austria, on an old ground in the textile town of Borås, displayed all the bad luck that seems to attend an ill-managed affair: shots against the post, a disallowed goal, wonderful strength in defence and mediocrity in attack. It was a 2–2 draw, and at the press conference Winterbottom said that it was the team's own fault, and that if you get the chances you must score. On the same evening Brazil beat Russia 2–0. They introduced Pelé and their skills ran riot. The results meant that Brazil had qualified for the quarter-finals but that England and Russia were equal on points and had to play off.

Most of my cables at this time were about our paper's local hero Bobby Charlton, who had been dropped after a disastrous warm-up defeat in Yugoslavia. With Finney still injured, others demoralised and everyone tired, would the selectors recall him? They did not. They brought in other youngsters but not Charlton, and the match against Russia was as depressing as some of those twenty years later, when England failed to qualify for successive World Cups. Fumbling and bad luck continued. Chances were made but not taken, and Russia won 1–0 with a shot that bounced in off the post. At the press conference afterwards Winterbottom was snappy and flustered: he defended his punchless winger A'Court, I remember, on the grounds that 'he does a lot of spoiling'.

What difference Charlton might have made to this sorry tale is hard to say. His class, his shooting and his high-speed running at people were already there; but he was raw, and the truth is that England had excellent defenders but not enough creativity. Even before Munich the England selectors had made Johnny Haynes their playmaker. To the Manchester press he was a controversial figure who exemplified the way in which London newspapers wrote players up and influenced their careers. Bias in both north and south clouded the Haynes issue, just as it clouded the Glenn Hoddle issue thirty years later. The apocryphal on-field conversation between Hoddle and Peter Reid during a 1986 World Cup game has always seemed to me to be a classic of this genre.

Reid: What the fuck are you doing?
Hoddle: You've got to let me be creative.
Reid: Yes. Well, do it in their penalty area and not ours.

Hoddle did play too deep, and I think that the truth about Haynes is that although he had a creator's brain, because he took too long to get the ball on to his favoured left foot and lacked that necessary deadly acceleration, he could never at the highest levels of the game control the tempo. The finest teams all too often had a moment in which to recover. Again, although the England defenders were good at stopping the opposition they did not have many ideas going forward.

The lost Byrne and Edwards might of course have

supplied this quality in Sweden. Even so, when we come to consider the gap between English and foreign foot‐ball, I think that it is in this issue of creativity from the back that we will find it – and not just in the 1950s, but to this day.

Defeat was clearly an emergency, and warranted a phone call to the office. 'Where are you?' I was in the press centre at the Ullevi. They told me to stay on and contact Jimmy Murphy, because Wales had won a place in the quarter-finals and were flying in that afternoon to meet Brazil.

Cliff! What the fuck are you doing, Cliff?

We went out to the airport to meet them. Jimmy was in great form after the play-off victory over Hungary, which took place in a thunderstorm to the chants of exiles attacking the Hungarian government, but his Juventus star John Charles had a black eye and a heavy limp: the Hungarians had hacked him and he would not be able to play. That evening we went to their hotel in a village beyond the suburbs and Jimmy and his captain Dave Bowen asked me questions about each Brazilian attacker. Which foot does he favour? Does he go inside or outside? Which way does he turn when his back is to goal?

Jimmy's relationship with the Welsh players was one

of passion leavened by comedy. One of the best stories concerns an inside right named Reg Davies, who played for Newcastle United. He was to bc marked by Duncan Edwards in a game against England, and asked his manager for a private word.

'Jimmy,' he said, 'he's your player. How shall I play him?'

Jimmy pondered. 'Reg,' he said, 'keep out of his fucking way.'

Wales then as now had the problem of a few top-quality players, a few average and a few whose talents were below the international mean. To make the best of it Jimmy devised what he called a retreating defence. This was not so much a system of lines across the field as a funnel which packed the central areas but still had wide men ready to break. The funnel moved upfield and back and the different departments of the team stayed in contact with each other. The aim was not simply to enmesh superior teams but to strike counter-blows through the speed of the outside left Cliff Jones and the class of John Charles and the Swansea inside forward Ivor Allchurch. The team who had perfected this kind of falling-back defence were the multi-talented Austria of the mid-30s: when they recovered the ball they came out together with crisp passing movements and their centre forward Sindelar was a genius. Their coach was Jimmy Hogan, at more or less the same time that Jimmy Murphy met him in Paris. When Wales countered they perforce relied on longer passes, but I have often thought that Murphy must have remembered the old man's wisdom.

Once he had decided upon his system Jimmy did not confuse the players but stuck to it in all circumstances, even when Sweden, having qualified, played a weakened team against them. It got them three draws and a play-off victory, and they twice came from behind to achieve something.

They played Brazil in a half-empty stadium around which Jimmy's voice rang like a cracked foghorn. Brazil did the attacking and were enmeshed. Garrincha, the right-winger who terrorised the world, was ushered outside so that his centres crashed into the photographers or the side netting; Zagallo was held off; Mazzola was shackled; and Didi's probing passes became ever more hopeful lobs. Out came the Arsenal goalkeeper Jack Kelsey to make his catches. Two or three times the counter-attacks worked, most notably a few minutes after the start, when Cliff Jones was clean through but so amazed that he shot wide.

'Cliff! What the fuck are you doing, Cliff?' boomed the foghorn.

Ivor Allchurch was almost there in the second half, but Brazil won through Pelé's first international goal, a mishit effort that bounced before it went in.

All told, they had once again not looked like supermen.

Next morning I phoned the office and Jack Smith said, 'You'd better come back. Can you buy an air ticket?' We stayed over the weekend, which was the Swedish Midsummer's Eve, and went by flying boat to Copenhagen, and thence to Manchester. The next evening the Brazil versus France semi-final was on TV. Raymond Kopa, playing in the hole behind the French front men, did indeed put pass after pass through the Brazilian back four, but after twenty-seven minutes a diabolical tackle by Vava broke the French centre half's shin. France were down to ten men and the contest was over. Brazil ran out 5–2 winners and in the final they beat Sweden's veterans by the same score, whereupon history blazed their fame and Pelé's across the world.

PART SIX
Close Season

Journey's end

Our return to England was the end of an emotional journey, and of a phase of life, that had begun on the afternoon of the Munich crash. Things would be different now. In a few weeks we would be married and move into a better flat, and the job would not be a unique adventure but a routine that if I wanted to become a writer I would have to leave. I knew this but was not ready to face it. I was in a close season, that time when nothing happens but everything changes. After a few weeks I went to see Jimmy at Old Trafford and he did not talk about the future either, nor about the emotions of the time after Munich.

He talked about the World Cup and what it meant for tactics, which set me thinking in a more analytical way, so that if this book has an intellectual argument it is that United's story is linked to that of English football as a whole, but in a negative sense. For the most part football practice ignored what Busby and Murphy did, as it has ignored Ferguson, and has been the poorer for it. Ironically, the first commentator to grasp this was the old Arsenal man Bernard Joy.

A day or two after the Munich crash Joy wrote an article that Jack Smith took over the wire from the *Evening Standard*. He said that it would take United five years to recover, a prediction that would prove accurate to within a couple of months, but that for English football as a whole the situation was worse. There was now no example to follow, he said. The W formation was discredited, the Spurs push and run was about a particular group of men rather than a style; and the Wolverhampton long ball game could degenerate into the kick and rush. Where, he asked, was the way forward?

Post-mortems

Curiously, this was not a question that was asked after England's World Cup failures. Their dismissal from the tournament of 1950 had been seen as shaming but a fluke that happened on a field far away. I still remember the TV coverage of the 1954 finals, which revealed a glorious variety of styles and tactics: a treasury that television showed and then began to reduce, as people saw and copied. Scotland were humiliated in 1954 but England reached the last eight with displays that better team selections could have improved. It seemed to me and my friends that our football had not been seen at its actual best, so how could we know for sure what was wrong with it, or what was good and could be built on? We talked instead about the way the team was run.

That is why, when the journalists who had been in Sweden, or seen it on television, wrote their post-mortems on England's disappointing showing they did not hark back particularly to the damage caused by the Munich crash. They talked about poor management because millions of other people had seen the games on television, and the popular press had to reflect their feelings. They had to articulate dissatisfaction. The press found within itself the stirrings of a sensationalist power, first toyed with by men like Henry Rose, that decades later was to mortally wound Taylor, Hoddle, Keegan, Eriksson and McLaren.

Of course, some of this was good. The Selection Committee system *was* out of date, and when Alf Ramsey came along, his appointment urged by the papers, a manager with sole powers *did* make more effective team selections. But for the rest the papers said that English football was in decline, and had been for years, and left it at that, without many whys or hows or very much about what could be done about it. They did not even say that England could have been pragmatic and picked a one-off party of proven ballplayers, Old Uncle Stan Matthews and all, as they did in 1954 when they knew that they had to win a friendly against the world champions West Germany, and succeeded with a Matthews-Revie-Allen-Shackleton-Finney forward line.

This line-up was the best England attack I saw, even if only on television. Why nobody tried the same again I have never understood, any more than I understand why someone as brilliant as Dennis Viollet won only one England cap. Although having been in the theatre for forty-odd years, and seen overactors on the one hand and energy-less wankers on the other hailed as titans, of course I understand, but it goes hard, and it is why I cling to United. But nothing was deduced from either them or Tottenham, the most skilful teams of the 1950s, just as little had been learned from Chapman's Arsenal. Instead, club football became even more envious and tribal. The chronic under-performance of England teams was made to seem inevitable. Then when Alf Ramsey did something about it people rushed to the opposite extreme and behaved as though everything was perfect. Interestingly enough, Matt Busby's public utterances on these matters were invariably moderate. In his various ghosted interviews and autobiographies he never said that English football had declined, just that it had stood still while the rest of the world advanced.

Broken time

When we consider English football we should never forget that the game as we understand it began in the public schools and universities, whose business was to turn out an imperial governing class. Ideals of social responsibility and political worth were expressed through notions of sportsmanship: the game for the game's sake, self-sacrifice, devotion to a cause. It's not cricket, old chap. Play up, play up and play the game.

To Victorian headmasters like Arnold at Rugby and Thring at Uppingham, who made sport an important part of the curriculum, this moral aspect was the most important. It put healthy minds into healthy bodies. It was a way of conditioning young men through some-thing they enjoyed.

Some of these young men became football's first

administrators. They wrote the laws of the game and founded the Football Association, as others of their kind created rugby, hockey, tennis and other sports that began as recreations for a moneyed middle class. When football was taken by members of that class to the industrial north and Midlands it spread downwards into society as a whole. This was the very moment at which the workers had begun to win themselves days off and leisure time, and within a couple of decades football had become a spectator sport played by professionals. The gentlemen amateurs were delighted that their passion had taken hold, but tried to keep it within their notions of decency and the working man's place in the world. Their instinct was to ban professionalism altogether, but they could not.

The culture of the bung began early, in the late 1870s, when Scots working-class players, known as 'professors', were given jobs in Lancashire mills. When it became obvious that the northern clubs had the strength to break away the Football Association relented and allowed professionalism. The social classes held together, but at a price: hypocrisy, which it must be said was for the most part the fault of the game's administrators and the provincial businessmen who came to control the clubs.

An Edwardian working-class entertainer like Marie Lloyd could earn thousands in the music hall, but Billy Meredith could never be paid what he was worth on the field, because if he had been most of the smaller clubs would have been unable to compete. Equal access to competition was one of the tenets of public school sportsmanship, and it suited the clubs to pay it lip service. At the same time they imposed a maximum wage and disallowed freedom of contract. Working men were to be kept in their place. And the richer clubs paid bungs as often as not. It is ironic that a culture of corruption was institutionalised by the very thing that was supposed to end it: legal professionalism.

A further consequence of this moral confusion was the Football Association's quarrel with FIFA, which began in 1928 and was not resolved until after the war, over 'broken time' payments to amateurs. The best example of this are the Scandinavian teams against whom Matt Busby managed Great Britain in the 1948 Olympics. They were technically amateurs, but they received money for time lost from their jobs. In the 1920s the FA refused to countenance this, and insisted upon Victorian notions of honour. Again this is ironic. Amateurs like Harold Hardman had been able to play in professional teams because of their outside incomes; they drifted away after 1914 not because professional standards rose, but because work demands upon the middle class were heavier.

It was because of the broken time quarrel, which was an attempt to protect the pure amateurism of the Olympic Games, that the Football Association refused to send England teams to the first three World Cups in 1930, 1934 and 1938, so English football did not benefit from the experience of different ideas and conditions. What made this critical in the long run was the change in the offside law – the defining event of modern football – which had taken place in 1925.

In the mid-nineteenth century each public school played football according to its own rules. For a match between, say, Eton and Westminster there would be a meeting beforehand to decide which rules would be used. The first common code was agreed among Cambridge undergraduates in 1848, and became the basis of the Football Association's rules when it was formed in 1863. The notion of offside existed at all, I read some-where, because at Charterhouse the game had been played in the cloisters. Boys would hide behind a buttress ahead of the play and sneak out at a favourable moment to score. A friend of mine who teaches at Eton and has been much involved in their field game, has never heard this story, so maybe it's apocryphal. What is certain is that the original offside law resembled that of rugby union, where a player must be behind the ball, but this was changed in 1867, so that a player with three oppon-ents ahead of him was onside.

When this rule was adopted more or less every player ran all over the field, to chase the ball or to support the man in possession, a tactic known as backing up. By 1925, when the rule was changed, complex posi-tional specialities and styles of play had evolved. Men stayed in defensive positions and were called backs. Then others filled the gap between the chasers and the backs and were called halfbacks. By the mid-1880s illegally paid northern teams had overtaken gentlemen amateurs like Oxford University and Old Etonians, and the game was acquiring a shape that we would recognise today. There was the traditional short passing of the Scots and the direct wing play of many English clubs. There were centre forwards as different as the bustling Harry Hampton of the Edwardian Aston Villa, and the shrewder, deeper-lying organiser John Goodall, who under the first real football manager, William Sudell, a rogue who called himself Major and eventually ran off to Australia, schemed Preston North End to the League and Cup double in 1888.

And as British businessmen, administrators, seminarists, sailors on shore leave, clerks in banks and fitters installing machinery took their game abroad, it spread into other cultures and came in its turn to express them. By the 1920s the Brazilians were already flamboyant, the Austrians bourgeois methodical, the Spaniards harsh in the tackle, the Uruguayans full of grace and virtuosity.

In all these styles and places players tried to attack and score as many goals as they could and, as often as not, particularly before 1914, the best player in the team, the most variously gifted, was the man at the centre of things, the centre half – like Charlie Roberts at Old Trafford and the great Colin Veitch of Newcastle United.

Then in the 1920s another Newcastle player, Billy McCracken, fifteen times an Irish international, invented the offside trap. He played right back and was first capped in 1902, so maybe it was to save his ageing legs that he stepped upfield to catch entire forward lines offside. His trick was copied everywhere. It was a mockery of sporting spirit and the history of the game so far. It enraged the public and the FA had to respond. They came up with the two-man offside law, and the rest of the world followed suit.

The W formation

It took time for people to adjust to the new law, and for a season or two attackers ran riot. They had after all been given yards of space in front of goal. In 1926/7 George Camsell scored fifty-nine goals for Middlesbrough, and in the following season Dixie Dean hit sixty for Everton. By then, however, Herbert Chapman, whose Huddersfield Town team of the early 1920s was the last glorious expression of the old football, had become manager of Arsenal. He and his inside forward Charlie Buchan are credited with the simple idea that restored some sort of balance: the withdrawal of the centre half to a defensive role as a third fullback.

The disadvantage of this system was that it left a gap in midfield where the centre half had been, and this was remedied by the withdrawal of the inside forwards, so that the five attackers played not so much in a line as in a W formation, the name which came to be given to this entire style of play.

The wingers and the centre forward in a W formation tended to stay upfield, where they were man-marked by the opposing backs and centre half, and in the midfield the inside forwards and wing halves were four against four. This is why individual contests became so vital. A winger who beat his man could wreck the entire defence, as Stanley Matthews did so many times. It became more important for a defender to mark and tackle than to play a constructive ball, and because there was more space everywhere with a two-man offside law, wing halves needed to chase more.

In other words it became easier to be negative than to be positive. Because defenders stayed back and some forwards stayed up, the distances between players became greater. Teams came to use longer passes, hitting the ball up to the winger; the winger making ground and delivering crosses. Physical effort, hard running and the carrying of the ball by an inside forward became more important than elaborate passing movements.

In one fateful sense, of course, this was the crowds' delight. The English instinct has always been to attack, to make ground, to shoot first time like Steve Bloomer. English crowds revel in it. They want movement, pace and high-speed drama, all of which were inevitable in W-formation football, as were triumphs of directness like the 4–0 defeat of Italy in 1948.

When football restarted in 1946, and all people wanted to do was enjoy the peace, it was easy to overlook how hard it was for the different departments of most teams to stay in touch, how they tended, in Jimmy Murphy's phrase, to get strung out, and how, because skill at the back and at wing half had been neglected, they tried to join themselves up again with hopeful long balls.

What one might call the kick and rush.

'Lucky' Arsenal

What happened next outwitted everyone. Herbert Chapman, who launched the W formation, tried it for a year or two and then moved on. Chapman understood that when the rules favoured defenders the way to win was to lure them forward and create space behind them. The classic Arsenal played neither a W formation nor an offside game. They defended in depth, played a holding and passing game to draw teams forward, and counter-attacked. Their system continued into the 1950s, long after Chapman's death, and I actually reported games in which they played away from home with one lonely man up front. If a classic W-formation team lined up 3–2–2–3 Arsenal were more variable, although in full cry at home they were as near 4–2–4 as made no difference.

Between 1930 and 1939 Arsenal won the League five times and the Cup twice. They supplied seven members of the England team that beat the world champions Italy, and in a famous friendly at Highbury they beat FK Austria, managed by Hugo Meisl, which contained most of the Austrian national team. They were perhaps the best club team in Europe. Yet only one other English club attempted to copy their style of play, and that after 1945: Burnley, who used a dour version of it to get themselves out of the Second Division and into the 1947 Cup Final.

'Lucky' Arsenal were hated, but it was not for their success and their deliberate glamour alone. They were disapproved of because it was felt that their defensive style of play was unsporting. It was cynical. It wasn't trying to do your best at all times. The fact that it was visionary was not understood, not even twenty years later when people saw successful foreign teams doing the same thing as though it was brand new.

Catching up

What is easy to forget, or not to realise, is the pace of football's development in the rest of the world. The game was introduced into Brazil, for example, in 1896, but there were no professionals there until 1932; Uruguay allowed professionalism in the same year, and Chile in 1933, while Argentina had done so in 1931. Yet the South American Championship had been contested since 1916, and Uruguay had won the Olympics in 1924 and 1928, as well as the inaugural World Cup in 1930.

Austria, Hungary and Czechoslovakia allowed professionalism soon after the First War. France was next, followed in 1929 by Italy, who at once scoured Latin America for stars with Italian ancestry. Some Scandinavians are to this day what we might call broken time professionals: was not Manchester United's Blomqvist a bank clerk before he left Gothenburg for Italy? When the Romanians went to the first World Cup the players worked for English and American oil companies, and King Carol paid for their broken time; and from 1945 until the collapse of communism eastern European clubs were all in one way or another government subsidised.

When we consider such a patchwork of circumstances, the FA's 1928 stand over broken time payments seems uninformed and unsophisticated as well as moralising.

England played and won seven European internationals before 1914, against Austria, Hungary and Bohemia. They scored forty-eight goals and conceded seven. They did not play these teams again for twenty years. In 1930 they drew 0–0 with Austria, beat them 4–3 in 1932, and lost 1–2 in 1936. They lost to Hungary in 1934 and beat them in 1936. In 1934 Czechoslovakia, the old Bohemia, were runners-up in the World Cup and beat England 2–1, but in 1937 England won 5–4.

Until they met Spain in Madrid in 1929 and were beaten 4–3 England had played twenty-three matches against continental sides and won them all. Between Madrid and the war they won eleven, drew three and lost five. They did not play a Latin American team until they beat Chile 2–0 in the 1950 World Cup. Scotland did not play a continental team until 1929, and Wales until 1933, when Jimmy Murphy was in their 1–1 draw with France, and afterwards sought out Jimmy Hogan. In 1934 Wales won the British Championship, and France were knocked out of the World Cup finals by Austria, who took fourth place.

The rate of catch-up is obvious, and British attitudes were insular. Yet England did *play* the leading teams of Europe, and at the end of the 1930s were on a par with them. After the war England's team was excellent, but when it aged nemesis was swift. One reason for this is startling. It is that during the war British football was virtually shut down. Teams played in regional leagues and their players were taken into the services. But on the continent much football continued, particularly when the greater part of the land mass was under German control.

Sepp Herberger – his predecessor Otto Nerz was a Jew who died in a concentration camp – managed Germany at the 1938 World Cup, in wartime internationals against neutrals, conquered nations and allies, and through chaos into the 1954 World Cup. Neutrals on the edges of Hitler's Europe played each other as well as countries within the Axis. The German system did not come from nowhere. It was forged in the war years, and when their captain Fritz Walter lifted the 1954 World Cup in Berne he was an international footballer of vast experience.

In wartime France, Norway and Poland league football

stopped, but it never did so in Denmark and Hungary. Austria, Bulgaria, Holland, Finland and Czechoslovakia lost one season each, Romania two and Belgium three. In Italy there was no league in 1944 and 1945, and in Germany itself from 1945 to 1947. But plans, experiments and the actual profession of football had by and large continued, and when the game restarted it was obvious who had thought about it the most.

Continental nations had never been persuaded by the change in the offside law to give up their passing games, because they did not believe that man-to-man marking was the only way to prevent goals. What attackers wanted was space, and when continental centre halves were withdrawn it was as often as not to defend an area of space and not mark a particular man. This is called zonal defence. If the ball was played out more slowly than in England, foreigners did not care. They had never been committed to speed for speed's sake anyway, but to keeping the team together, as the old British coaches had taught them. It was the killer ball that had to be quick.

If this sounds like a description of Alex James organising Arsenal counter-attacks in the 1930s that is no coincidence.

What continental coaches had worked towards during the war, and produced soon after, were ways of having an entirely free man at the back: the Swiss 'bolt', the Italian 'sweeper', the German 'libero'. This man, often the best in the team, would have the time to close down space and the freedom to initiate the counter. Of course, the teams of Italy's historic cities, who in Brian Glanville's memorable phrase 'used to fight each other with mercenaries and now do so with footballers', soon donned belts as well as braces and used markers in front of sweepers, but that is a particular story, and it did not stop them being football's hothouses for half a century.

Only the Hungarians, the hustlers who enter a swing-door behind you and come out in front, had in the post-war years an inspired attacking notion: the deep-lying centre forward, which at Wembley was to kill the W formation.

In the 1950s

English football did not want to be overtaken, of course, and it is a paradox that at the time of its supposed lowest ebb, when I reported for the *Sunday Express*, there were lively experiments and achievements at club level. With the marvellous Jimmy McIlroy at inside forward Burnley were great counter-attackers. Newcastle United played an arrowhead formation, with Jackie Milburn at the tip. Blackpool and Sunderland filled their W formations with ballplayers. West Bromwich Albion, who won the Cup in 1954, were coached for a time by Jesse Carver, who had worked in Milan and brought with him new ideas about fitness and training as well as a sophisticated passing game that used a withdrawn centre forward. Arsenal made pioneering trips to play friendlies in Brazil. The Spurs push and run team of 1951 was a miracle for a moment; Manchester City had their Revie plan; and for more than a decade Wolverhampton Wanderers played their specialised version of the W formation.

This fired a long ball out of defence to the wingers, who were fast, direct and the most advanced men in the team. The centre forward was a skill player and held the ball up when first-phase attacks had been rebuffed. Wolves had great strength, great running and great destructive power at half back. In floodlit friendlies they beat Racing Club of Buenos Aires, Spartak Moscow, Maccabi Tel Aviv, Honved, who fielded most of the Hungarian national team, and Real Madrid over two legs, although the heaviness of the Molyneux pitch did play a part. But they had been thrashed by the Busby Babes in full cry, and when they reached the European Cup they did not do well.

One of the most damaging effects of decline is that it alters perception. People want things to be better but they do not recognise what might make them so. They become convinced that their interests are best served by what is stifling them, and they unconsciously accept lower standards: as Winterbottom mistook the second-rate creativity of Johnny Haynes for the real thing.

I do not think that Matt Busby had the need to intellectualise these matters, but he did have very powerful instincts.

When he came down from Scotland to Manchester City he soon learned that there was something wrong in the lives of professional footballers. Because they were not treated with respect they did not behave with respect, to themselves or to their craft. He went with City to play a friendly in Prague, where they were beaten, and he saw another attitude. He could pick on a player's faults, and was famous for doing so when he analysed opposing teams, but I do not think that his head was full of tactics. He had been a great player, Jimmy always said, and his feet talked quicker than his tongue. But he knew sound sense when he heard it, as on the day he heard Jimmy Murphy lecture at the army rest camp in Bari.

Jimmy was very articulate about football. He thought and analysed and asked questions and discussed. He must have had a hundred questions for Jimmy Hogan, but I think that really they were all about the same thing: how did a team hold itself together as a unit?

This, I believe, was the substance of the lecture at Bari, and as soon as Matt heard it he knew what it meant.

Murphy cut through the problems of the W formation by ignoring them. He knew they were there but he was not interested. What he sought were the simple rhythms any formation must obey that would enable individuals and a team to respond to any given situation.

It was like the philosopher's stone, and Matt knew it, and with the incisiveness of a great leader he acted. He offered Jimmy a job there and then.

Busby's United made its first piece of history in February 1946, before a match against Bury in the wartime Football League North. They came out for the kickabout with three balls, one for the forwards to bang at the goalkeeper, one for the halves and one for the backs. Hitherto teams had come out with one, and taken turns. This is a far cry from today's elaborate warm-ups, but it was a singular statement of intent at a time when many people believed that players could see too much of the ball in training, and should concentrate on fitness.

Within months United had turned inside forwards like Carey and Aston into fullbacks, because they always believed that creativity should begin at the back.

Twelve years later Busby and Murphy could be seen to have set a huge example. They had shown that British pace and power could coexist with exquisite ballplay. They had created two very different teams, although both of them had attacked and defended as a unit. They knew, of course, when di Stéfano and Kopa and Hector Rial cut through them, that there was much more to learn, not least a dimension of psychology and concentration. And then their work was destroyed by a few moments on the Munich runway.

PART SEVEN
A Season Too Far

Return to Munich

Whatever Matt and Jimmy thought about United's own way forward, they projected an air of business-like confidence. Only in small explosions of frustration, as the season after Munich progressed, did Matt show the turmoil beneath his calm. He had accepted, in the weeks before the crash, management of the Scottish international side but had not been fit enough to take the team to Sweden. He had not resigned, however, and intended to pursue this outside responsibility. This seems to me the expression of a hope against hope that United would bounce back to the top in one go and everything be normal again — they had, after all, been offered and accepted an honorary place in the European Cup. So they would be there again, jousting with the champions.

Jimmy's assurance, in hindsight, was more genuine and relaxed. It was as though he felt that his getting the team to Wembley, and Wales to the quarter finals, had given him status in the eyes of the public; and that having decided not to leave United, he was content to stand to one side and watch Matt set the pace of recovery. If he was no longer raging it was because he knew that his energies had changed. He was no longer the demon workaholic who had coached the reserves in the mornings, done remedial work in the afternoons, worked with the kids on Tuesday and Thursday evenings, and on other nights gone scouting.

It left him and the club with a problem, of course: if he was less and less a tracksuited coach, how could he realise his ideas on the pitch?

Johnny Aston was brought in to oversee the youth players, and when after eighteen months injuries stopped Wilf McGuinness playing, he became a coach. After a while Jimmy did embark for one last time upon the scouting trail, the football masterpiece of which was the signing of George Best, whom every other club thought too small to make a player, and the social classic the hours spent tinkling on a pub piano in Maidstone, to get the confidence of the locals and discover what he could about David Sadler's character and family. As before, the boys were made to learn a trade, in case their football failed them. Four of the team that won the European Cup were the products of this last hurrah and a fifth man, Bobby Noble, was a great fullback who won a Championship medal but after thirty-three games lost his career in a car crash.

Altogether, although things seemed unaltered, there had been a sea change in Murphy's relationship with Matt. They were fifty years old and had expected ten years of success. But what they had to do was start again, without their original energy and optimism. From the moment Jimmy turned down Arsenal and whatever other offers he had, he and Matt were stuck with each other. In the eyes of the people they were heroic. They were the original dreamers of the dream, the yearning that was greater than ever. Surely they would not rest until the quest was done?

It was just that, for them to succeed, Matt's best friend and confidant now had to be Louis Edwards.

The pre-season tour to Germany in the early autumn of 1958 was the first time Big Louis was powerfully in evidence and made efforts to get to know the journalists. It was obvious by then that the London offices intended to build up their own men, and that there would never again be a northern constellation like that before Munich. The trend was for less measured and more juicy stories, and one of those who provided them was the *Daily Mail*'s Jack Wood, an overweight, chuckling, public-school sort of rogue who was only too happy to crack an afternoon bottle of champagne with Big Louis. They understood one another, and Big Louis told Jack how United had been badly underinsured before Munich, and how their finances were not as healthy as everyone liked to assume.

Next day it was all in the *Mail*. Louis sidled into the hotel bar like an ashamed Just William, if such a thing is possible, whereas beaming Jack had no shame at all. His other side, needless to say, was a ludicrous British war-film-style sentimentality: the fat boy with unexpected feelings. On the boat train he had described for about half an hour how he and his ex-girlfriend had spent the evening they split up. They discussed what dogs they would have owned if they had stayed together.

'I don't suppose I'll have one at all now,' he concluded, with definite moisture in his eye.

The crossing was rough, steep seas in harsh sunshine, and at Ostend we discovered that the bookings were split between two trains, with the journalists on the one that left early, so that next morning David and I sat in the dining car and wrote descriptions before we got to Munich of how we arrived there at Matt's side, and of the huge emotions. Then we arrived, waited to meet him off his train and phoned our stories. They both made our respective front pages. The *Evening News* even carried a photograph of Matt and me walking together, although the caption did not identify me.

Willy Meisl, journalist brother of Hugo, who had managed Austria before the war and engaged Jimmy Hogan as his coach, came to watch United train. He was elderly, with a stick, a beret and a loden coat, an old-time café intellectual, and Matt and Jimmy showed him great respect. He watched for a few minutes and said that United weren't fit yet and would be beaten. He was right, and they were, by a combined Bayern-1860 side. The reception for United was beer-hall-friendly with an undertone of resentment and disdain. On a trip to the Chiemsee we ate at a hotel where a little, plump, smiling guest took on all-comers at table tennis. He beat one or two of the players, who did not realise that it was a challenge, and then Jack Crompton saved the day, affecting uncertainty but winning with an amazing show-off shot from between his legs. But the weather was thundery and we were edgy and at the banquet Bill Foulkes riled me and I threw a glass of wine in his face. We made up on the terrace outside and on the train next day played cards all the way to Hamburg.

The hotel was on the Alster. We arrived around midnight. The players were packed off and everyone else pronounced themselves ready for bed. Then over a nightcap Jack Wood suggested that it would be a pity

to miss the Reeperbahn, and we took a taxi. We had
no sooner got out of it than we bumped into Matt,
Jimmy and Big Louis, staring intently at the prostitutes in the windows. Jimmy cackled with laughter,
Matt was a bit put out, and Louis was again Just William,
but this time with a hint of defiance. True to form,
Jack Wood was the only one of the party to avail
himself of the facilities, which he described in detail
over breakfast.

It was in Hamburg that Big Louis decided one evening
that dry Martinis would be in order and Matt concurred.
The hotel barman was not sure how to make them, and
let me behind the bar to do it, which added to Jimmy's
sense of me as a young man with a classical education.
Two Hamburger SV officials were in attendance, and
said that they had already booked saunas for the following
morning. I doubt that at this time there was a single
sauna in the whole of Greater Manchester.

The terraces of Hamburg's huge new municipal
stadium had been made by piling up bomb rubble, and
from the press box at the top we saw a rainswept game
in which Hamburger SV were the more muscular team
and won 2–0. Their centre forward Uwe Seeler, who
had just broken into the West German team, was a
battering ram, and United's centre half Ron Cope was
taken off with a gashed head, to appear in the press box
and sit between David and me. He gave an involuntary,
muttered running commentary. 'Go on, Freddie! Hard
luck, son! Go on!'

Banned from Europe

The German friendlies had sharpened the players and in their first ten League games they lost only twice, once when injury reduced them to ten men at West Ham, and scored twenty-seven goals. But they conceded fourteen, the statistic which by the end of the season was the most significant. Morale was good, however, and the first real disappointment, especially for our sports desk, came when the chairman Harold Hardman leaked to David Meek the news that, because of opposition within the game's hierarchy, United had been told that if they took up their invitation to play in the European Cup they would be banned from the League.

When Chelsea were champions they had heeded the League's advice and withdrawn from the inaugural European Cup. United had ignored it and gone ahead, and this legally correct decision against them was the League's revenge. United had tried to negotiate, but a meeting of League chairmen went against them. On the one hand United could not complain; on the other one sees not only envy but a profound unwillingness to look into the future.

What worried Jack Smith was that the story had been leaked to the *Evening News* and not our paper, either because Harold Hardman might not like me or because of the authority that Arthur Walmsley assumed in his columns. I think that there was some truth in this, but that on the day Hardman acted on impulse. He certainly took Busby and the club officials by surprise. David had stayed late at the ground one morning, Hardman was hopping mad and thought that enough was enough, and spoke out.

United backed down, but saved face and maintained their European pretensions by playing their designated opponents, the Swiss team Young Boys of Berne, in friendly matches on the days appointed. Later in the season they arranged a floodlit friendly with FK Austria – who arrived by train. I remember, because Busby took me to meet them at the station.

Worldliness defused the Hardman episode, although I believe it still festered. The leak was another of Busby's grievances against Hardman, and the behaviour of the League and the chairmen of lesser teams an early instance of the attitudes which thirty-odd years later impelled the big clubs to form the Premier League. Martin Edwards, I am sure, did not forget.

A record fee

The week before the first Swiss friendly Busby startled everyone and bought Albert Quixall from Sheffield Wednesday for the then British record transfer fee of £45,000. I say startled because one might have expected

United to build from the back and buy a defender or two, and because Quixall was never precisely a United kind of player. He was a brilliant high-speed dribbler and inter-passer who was inclined to disappear on a bad day, and he never got a grip on a game, nor slowed it down in order to strike quickly, in the way that United's creative men do to this day. He was twenty-four years old, had already been picked and discarded by England, and was generally regarded as a marvellous but half-realised talent. He was an amusing person, a bit of a card with contradictory, angelic looks.

The transfer was an on-off story over two or three days and the fact is that Busby did not conduct it with his customary decisiveness. He made the enquiry, went to Sheffield, was startled by the price and stalled. The Wednesday secretary-manager Eric Taylor, meanwhile, had leaked the story to the press. Busby returned to Manchester, was discouraged by Harold Hardman, and sought advice from Louis Edwards.

Matt had been introduced to Louis Edwards by the theatre manager Tommy Appleby, and when United went on an American trip in 1952 Big Louis was also aboard the *Queen Mary* and is said to have sent over bottles of champagne. At the theatre he and Matt would slip out for a natter if the play bored them, and there would be Saturday evening dinners at the Bridge Inn at Prestbury, at that time the smartest little restaurant in the area. By the mid-50s Louis lived in a huge house at Alderley Edge and the meat business he ran with his brother was at its height: they had extensive public authority contracts to supply schools, and not for twenty years did journalists sniff out the questionable ways in which many of them had been won. When he chose, Louis could talk about the meat business in almost poetic terms. I remember one conversation I had with him about refrigerated vending machines that was almost utopian in its vision of an easy-shopping future.

At what point Matt hit upon the notion of controlling the club through a director who would do his bidding nobody knew. But he did, and it was breathtaking, and Big Louis was the destined man. From his own point of view Louis Edwards was flattered to serve the charisma. He actually believed in easy shopping, and he passionately believed in the dream. His pleasure in the team was infectious, and it took a long time for anything to turn sour.

All this and more churned in the emotions of the Albert Quixall transfer, not least Matt's power instinct to get rid of the post-Munich buys Crowther and Taylor. Crowther was dropped after the Munich friendly in favour of a rampant Wilf McGuinness, and although he played another game or two he was soon sold to Chelsea. This made sense, but Ernie Taylor could have given some service. Jimmy tried to involve him in coaching the kids but Ernie was a cynical little pro and did not care that this was an attempt to save him. Matt wanted him out and bought a much younger forward to replace him. Some say that he was influenced in his choice of Quixall by his son-in-law Don Gibson. Gibson had started at United but been transferred to Sheffield Wednesday after his marriage, and the loss of his first-team place. It is out of character that Matt would be influenced in this way, but no more so than his wobble over the deal.

Big Louis Edwards did not wobble, apart, I daresay, from his impressive jowls. He strengthened Matt's resolve and told him to think big and do what he wanted.

Maybe, who knows, he guaranteed the money in case of overdraft. Albert Quixall became a United player, and on the evening of the transfer was grabbed by Granada TV for interviews. Through a friend I got into the studio and talked to him. He was an unusual, attractive mixture of an airy withdrawn-ness and the blunt. I think that playing for United proved hard for him, and that it was his ability to be private that sustained him.

'He'll quicken it all up,' Jimmy Murphy said to me, with a flicked glance to see how I was taking it.

'Yes,' I said.

He changed the subject. Like me I think he hoped that would happen, but feared that it wouldn't always.

Interlaken

Quixall made his debut against Tottenham Hotspur on a windy day and a bumpy pitch, and did not have much effect upon a spoiling draw. We went from Old Trafford to the station, the first stage of our journey to Switzerland for the friendly against Berne, and at the bookstall Matt bought the football papers. In our running reports and summaries both David and I had said that Quixall was disappointing and in the dining car Matt lost his temper with us. He suddenly shouted that our reports were a disgrace and that for my information Quixall had been told to be more forward, whereas I had said that he was wasted and made no impression upon big men. There was a shocked hush at this outburst. One could hear the cutlery jingle. The players had seen him lose his temper before, not least when the Babes had played cards for big money, but never at the press or semi-outsiders.

Interlaken in late September was rainy when we arrived, sunny at other times, and nippy in the evenings. We stayed in a big old hotel called the Beau Rivage and the players trained on the ground of the local Interlaken FC. There were railings around the pitch and a tiny pavilion, and the players were mostly waiters from the hotels. Their officials came to meet our sleeping car, which had been tacked on to a local train, and when United held a drinks party for them in the hotel Matt made a typical little speech in which he said, 'You're only a small club but you've got a big idea.'

It says a lot about how much I respected my first wife, and how blasé I was about my job, how really I should have given it up after the World Cup and gone freelance, that I concurred with her idea that she should make her own way to Switzerland, stay at a hotel nearby and go to the match. The World Cup had whetted her appetite and she liked to watch the training. When Matt heard about this from Jimmy he insisted that she stay at the Beau Rivage and go to the game on the team bus: to my knowledge she is the only woman to have done this with United, certainly in that epoch. She already knew David and various players, of course: I still ghosted for Bobby Charlton and he would come to our flat.

It was a long drive to the game, along the Lake of Thun and past its medieval castle to the Wankdorf Stadium (jokes from Fred Goodwin and Harry Gregg), which had been the scene of Germany's World Cup win over Hungary. The man next to me in the press box reeked of garlic more than anyone I have ever experienced. He was not a working journalist but a retired local, and gave a Ron Cope-style muttered commentary: in particular on the crunching tackles, because although I would not say that the Young Boys were the roughest team I ever saw, they came close.

My neighbour had nothing to do but exclaim, but I was working twice. Jack Wood had wended his cheery way again, the *Express* had sent a Manchester reporter who covered the Third Division North, and because the game was not competitive some other papers were unrepresented. The *News Chronicle* had asked me to cover for them. This led to the silliest mistake I made in journalism, even including the time I wrote for the *Guardian* the obituary of an actor who wasn't dead. That was the *Guardian*'s fault because they said that they would check but didn't, but the Wankdorf Stadium was all mine.

United were kicked out of the match 2–0 and feeling in the press box was high. What with the Swiss tackles and the garlic I was not concentrating, and when my phone rang I assumed that it was the *Evening Chronicle* and dictated my next-day summary. There would be another call from the *News Chronicle*. When it came I realised that it was our own London copy room. The first call had been the *News Chronicle* and I had sent them the wrong report. Jack Wood, hearing me dictate the same summary twice, realised what had happened and laughed so much that he had to wipe away tears. When I had almost finished my dictation I had the idea that saved me: I asked the London switchboard to put me through to the *News Chronicle* in Manchester.

World Cup 1958: (*above*) press card; (*below*) cable card

No. 861   Expires 31. 7. 1958

Name of bearer MR. KEITH DEWHURST

Signature of bearer Keith Dewhurst.

Visiting SWEDEN

ALL CLASSES
Valid for telegrams adressed to

"KEMNEWS LONDON"

(Kemsley Newspapers Ltd.
Kemsley House Grays In
Road London W.b.1)

FOR THE GREAT NORTHERN TELEGRAPH
COMPANY LTD.

This card is valid only when it contains the
signature of the bearer.

The right is reserved to withdraw at any time
the privileges conferred by this card, and the
bearer agrees to surrender this card upon its
expiry, or at the request of any officer of the
Company.

Requests for renewal or amendment of this
card may be made to any of the Company's
offices.

(*Above*) Brazil 1 Wales 0, World Cup Quarter-final, 23/6/1958. Altafina (aka Mazzola) (*left*) and Zagallo congratulate the scorer Pele; (*Below*) Mentioned in dispatches

Evening Gazette

From   A. L. JAMES,
MIDDLESBROUGH

To   Mr J. Goulden,
Evening Chronicle,
Manchester.
18th June, 1958.

         I thought you would like to know how pleased we have been here with Keith Dewhurst's stories from Sweden.

         My sporting colleagues, who are generally hard to satisfy, have been most impressed - especially by today's message.

         Considering Keith Dewhurst's short experience, it is a remarkable achievement. I should like to congratulate him - and you on picking him for the job !

From me the same. Reader Reaction very good too - and circulation Dept.

Regards,

AL J

Switzerland, 1958: (*Above*) Keith
Dewhurst in Zurich air terminal;
(*Right*) Albert Quixall (*centre*)
and Matt Busby at Interlaken;
(*below*) 'Hey up, lad':
Joe Armstrong

Players in the United power game:
(*left to right*) Les Olive, Denzil Haroun, Matt Busby, Louis Edwards

Old Trafford, the theatre of their dreams: (*Above*) Munich mural and Matt's statue, 2008; (*Below*) From the air, the monument in the post–industrial landscape

Legends: Denis Law (*above*) scores a mid–air goal against Fulham in 1967 and (*below*) Eric Cantona expostulates against Everton in 1996

Keith Dewhurst (*above*) in rehearsals at the Crucible Theatre, Sheffield, May 1975; (*below*) at home in London today

The old men at the end of their odyssey: Jimmy Murphy and Matt Busby coax their men home before extra-time in the European Cup Final, 29/5/1968

Next day I did not take the train with the team. My wife and I went into the mountains and flew home from Zurich. It was the only time Jack Smith was annoyed with me. I should have stayed with the team, and if anything had happened on the way back, and I had not been there to report it, I would have lost my job. 'I know,' I said. 'Do we gather from this,' said Arthur Walmsley in jovial mood, 'that you really do want to write scripts?'

Next day United played City at Maine Road and I stood with Arthur on the concourse outside the main stand, which was a time-honoured place for sporting characters to see and be seen, and for emboldened readers to come up and discuss the red-hot topics of the day. One of Arthur's regulars was a particularly intense small-time Jewish businessman, a City fanatic whom I was amused to meet because he was always writing to the Friday letters column. His reiterated phrase was <u>THERE IS NO SUBSTITUTE FOR SKILL</u>, in capitals and underlined, and Arthur would print one of his efforts every six weeks or so.

Years later there was a curious sequel, when Arthur and Eric Todd were invited to the businessman's wedding. He would have been in his late fifties. Arthur and Eric hummed, hawed, consulted one another and at length agreed. When they went they were the only guests.

What's wrong with United?

This game against City was the second in a ten-match run in which United won once, drew three times and lost six, scoring a mere eleven goals against twenty-three conceded. They were disjointed and disorganised and nothing would go right. The return match against Young Boys was won 3–0, so they would have progressed had it been a real European Cup tie, but it was not, and there was a lot more nasty tackling as well. An injury-hit team was hammered 4–0 at Wolverhampton, who led the League, and a full-strength one bamboozled by Tom Finney, playing as a scheming centre forward, when Preston North End won at Old Trafford. Everyone assumed that events would change but they did not. After another week or two Jack Smith asked me to get an interview with Billy Foulkes, the captain, and ask him what was wrong.

The problem of the travelling reporter was that he could become closer to the team than to the paper. Alf Clarke did. Tommy Jackson did, but with a less obvious display of bias. David Meek never did, at the beginning. His father had been a distinguished local journalist and on the board of York City, and David, who was never much into football before he was given the job, was brought up to behave with an easy detachment. It is an amusing irony that today, in retirement but with many pleasant responsibilities at Old Trafford, he really is close to the club and very discreet about it.

Unlike David I got much too close almost at once. I was a United supporter. They were my passion. I became entangled with Jimmy Murphy and all the things he told me. I was too close to his view of things and too close to someone like Bill Foulkes, whom I knew to have raw nerves under his coal miner's hardness, and whom I did not wish to embarrass. Because Jimmy had picked my brains about the Brazilians I fancied my judgement of the game. I knew that Bert Whalley, and not Matt Busby, had actually signed most of the Babes, and that Matt hadn't even seen some of them until they were United players.

What I should have done was to have had a chat with Matt and got some quotes. But I knew what he would say. He would say what he had said ten years before: that it was a loss of rhythm, and would soon come right. The first time I had believed it, but this time I didn't. 'You build from the back,' Jimmy Murphy had drummed into me, and Matt wasn't doing that. He was hoping to be saved up front by Albert Quixall.

Being the travelling reporter was a dream come true but really I was a fan and still am, and should never have done it. Things mattered too much. I said to Jack Smith that I would leave Bill Foulkes alone and write a couple of articles entitled WHAT'S WRONG WITH UNITED? Tactical analysis. Where Matt Busby was wrong. Jack seized on the idea and advertised it. The articles were silly but accurate after their arrogant fashion, as though football was an intellectual exercise and not a matter of cajoling and inspiring confidence. Word came back that Matt was not best pleased, and I went to Old Trafford to talk to him.

It was one of the last days on which he went out in a tracksuit. I sat with him in the referee's room as he finished dressing, which was when I first noticed his elegant shoes. Then he drove me to his house for a cup of tea. It was a curious conversation because I defended not what I had said but my right to say it, and Matt knew that he had no actual authority over me. He said that he did not want to use his ghosted articles to discuss what was wrong with the team, or to point out why in his opinion I was mistaken. I said that the paper could not ignore it when things went wrong. People in pubs and offices had their opinions and expected us to reflect them. Matt said that I was a young man and should try to learn. I said I was trying to. Mrs Busby fussed around us with biscuits.

What I had written was impulsive, but by insisting upon my right to say it I had unintentionally wrecked the spin-doctoring and made things inconclusive. The fact is that after this conversation there was a defined distance between me and Matt, but that he engaged me much more seriously. I lost my nervousness of saying what I thought to him, and he would ask me a lot more questions. He invariably picked my brains about the shows we were taken to on away-game Friday nights. He was a good judge of entertainment theatre, and liked it to be well drilled. He was as uneasy with my education, I guess, as I was with his self-control.

The next game saw United beaten 6–3 at Bolton in an utterly ludicrous encounter. In those days a referee could play on in fog provided he could see both goals and touchlines from the centre spot. This was said to be the case at Burnden Park, where there was haze before the kick-off. We saw the first couple of goals from the press box and then true fog descended. Crowd noise may or may not have indicated a score. We did see a strip of touchline and an occasional glimpse of United's new right winger Warren Bradley, but nothing more, and stewards would run from the gloom from time to time to say that a goal had been scored, and who, according to some name shouted from the field, had scored it.

It was a joke, and Matt shook his head when I bumped into him in the passage beneath the stand. The twinkle in his eye was for the fact that I'd funked the team bus because I thought the players would give me a bad time over the articles. 'Come back with us,' he said. I did. There were a few snarls but I probably deserved them.

David and I were still part of the family and animosities were not allowed to fester. There were cliques but they were social, more like natural friendships, and what Matt had inculcated was tolerance and looking out for one another. When I heard around the traps that journalists were talking about Dennis Viollet and another woman it seemed common sense to warn him. When the teenaged Johnny Giles travelled for the first time he did not have a friend and was left in the hotel, so David and I took him to the pictures. Misdeeds were noted but allowed to lie, as when Colin Webster clouted his wife in a fight. By chance my wife's hairdresser was married to the reserve fullback Tommy Heron, and they would come to our house. Nothing controversial was ever discussed. It was again what Matt had inculcated.

A winning run

Within a couple of weeks everyone was smiling again. There was a streaky home win over Luton Town and then a brilliant display at Birmingham, who were beaten 4–0 in true United style. There had been two significant changes. Joe Carolan, a twenty-one-year-old Irish player who had been with the club for two seasons, replaced Ian Greaves at left back and Warren Bradley came in at outside right. Bradley had played for Bishop Auckland and joined United as an amateur after Munich. Then he moved his schoolteaching job to Manchester and turned pro. He was small, fast and direct, and the forward line now read Bradley-Quixall-Viollet-Charlton-Scanlon. There was tremendous pace here, but Viollet's conducting of the orchestra from a withdrawn centre forward position was the key. With Goodwin an attacking wing half and McGuinness more defensive it was almost a 4–2–4. How far this had been urged by Murphy I am not sure, but it reflected a lot of his ideas, particularly the centre forward as schemer, as Sindelar had been for Hogan's Austria. Altogether, in this third and most successful quarter of their season, United put together a sequence of eleven League wins and one draw. They scored thirty-six goals and conceded sixteen, and rose to second place in the table.

When the club was happy so were the reporters. Our routine was easy. We would go to the ground most mornings and use our press-box phones to send our stories. Underneath the stand was an echoing world of girders, metal fencing and gates. At half-time the crowd could see through and watch the teams troop out, but on weekdays the gates were left open. David Meek and I once kicked a ball through them with Bobby Charlton, his half-volleys swerving as they came back at us.

One incident of this period was a classic of Matt's Gemini style. Stan Crowther was sold to Chelsea, recouping some of Quixall's fee, and almost at once faced United at Stamford Bridge. The game was the one blinder I saw Harry Gregg play, and during it Crowther put up his foot and gashed Bobby Charlton's shin. Then because he hadn't moved house yet he travelled back with us on the train. There were scowls and a muttered 'It was deliberate, you know' from Billy Foulkes. But Matt, who had just dumped the boy without mercy, went out of his way to have a kind and settling word with him.

Giant-killed

In the Cup United were drawn against the winners of a replay between Norwich City and Swindon Town, and both David and I were sent to Norwich to see the game. They were both Third Division teams but Norwich won well against a much cruder Swindon. On the train back I started to write my first TV drama commission, a two-part story for a Granada thriller series called *Shadow Squad*. All TV was live, of course, and the demand for material was voracious. Writers could learn as they went along and ascend the ladder from shorter to longer shows, and from serials to series, and eventually single plays. As often as not the directors and producers were people with wide experience of life, theatre and films, and their advice was practical: a far cry from television today, and its arrogant but confused executives. As I took these first steps along another road United's run continued. There was some terrific high-speed football, and over Christmas they beat Aston Villa twice.

There was a press room under the Villa Park Stand, and in it Kemsley had its own phone. It was kept in a locked box and had to be taken up to the press seats and plugged in. When I reported the Cup Semi-Final in April someone had been there to unlock the box and I was assured that this would again be the case. But when the phone rang at ten to three it was still in the box, which no one had come to open, and I had to hire one. When I explained to Jack Smith he had a weary smile. Maybe, surmised Arthur Walmsley, ever ready with helpful satire, the mistake was that it was never actually our phone in the first place.

Ten days later we went in the coach to King's Lynn, where we stayed at a hotel on the big old market square. There were stalls and naphtha flares and it seemed Pickwickian almost, an older, more rural and robust sort of England. At the match next day the pitch was frozen and the crowd and the local press in a high old state of excitement, as though they already knew that a bit of history was in the offing. I had written in my preview that Norwich were the very type of a giant-killing team, because they were well balanced and had two or three players, typified by the centre forward Roy Bly, who were a distinct class above the division in which they were playing. But I forecast a United win.

'Great tipster you are!' chaffed Harry Gregg on the way home, after Norwich had beaten him three times without reply.

In fact the early chances had fallen to United and they could have scored two or three before Norwich, fearless on the hard ground, swept them aside. We returned for dinner to the hotel at King's Lynn, where the waiters could not hide their smirks, and then home in cold so bitter that ice formed inside the metal roof of the coach.

Even this numbing defeat seemed to have been shrugged off, as did Bill Foulkes's request to be dropped and relieved of the captaincy because he was mentally worn out. After an exciting 4–4 draw with Newcastle there were more League victories. Tottenham were defeated at White Hart Lane by a marvellous Bobby Charlton goal, hit on the volley from a long pass forward by McGuinness, and then the League leaders Wolverhampton were beaten 2–1 at Old Trafford. With a successful run in, it seemed, the gamble could be landed. United could surge ahead and snatch the title.

Only six shots at goal

The next match was against Arsenal at Highbury, and there was an unseasonable change in the weather: overnight greyness and rain turned to a low, dazzling sun and a breeze that made a muddy pitch hard and bouncy. They were bad omens. United had always seemed to battle harder in poor weather, and Jimmy Murphy called the grey shadowless afternoons of October 'the ballplayer's light'. David and I went for our traditional Hyde Park stroll but it seemed odd to be without Bill Foulkes. When we got back to the shabby but friendly hotel in Lancaster Gate Walter Winterbottom had arrived, and Matt suggested that we join them for an aperitif.

A little horseshoe bar stuck out into the room. Matt and Jimmy were on one side, David and I on the other, and Winterbottom in the middle. There was football small talk. Then out of nothing Winterbottom said that he had been reading this absolutely fascinating book by Richard Hoggart. It was called *The Uses of Literacy* and was about the formation of cultural subgroups within the working class. Did any of us know anything about it?

There was a disbelieving silence. Winterbottom waited like an eager form master. Matt Busby's eyes looked at mine, and in a very direct way: this was unusual for him whoever a person was, but then he did realise that I was the only one of us who might have heard of Richard Hoggart, let alone read the book. Fortunately I had done both, and the day was saved. Jimmy almost chortled. There's my boy, said his smirk. Matt suavely introduced a more accustomed topic. The matter was never alluded to again.

After lunch someone went missing and we sat on the bus while Jack Crompton searched. Winterbottom, standing on the steps, said that when he played for United there had been a simple solution to this type of situation. The trainer shouted 'One!' and if the goalkeeper was present he said 'Yes,' and so on through all the shirt numbers.

'What number were you, Walter?' cried Wilf McGuinness from the back. 'Thirteen?'

He was speaking to the England team manager, who capped him later in the year, and a man who in the war had been a wing commander.

Highbury's halls were as marble as ever but the match was a disaster. Arsenal won 3–2 and United could not get the ball off them. Tommy Docherty and Arsenal's captain Dave Bowen played excellent possession football and United only scored at all because of Dennis Viollet's flair.

After the game George Swindin, who had been given the Arsenal managership when Jimmy turned it down, came into the press room and glowed with self-satisfaction. David and I left after that because once again we did not want to miss the bus, but this time it had not arrived and we waited in the street. Who should come up, on his way home, but Walter Winterbottom.

'Hello, boys!' he cried, and pulled from his pocket a

piece of paper on which he had pencilled notes. 'Do you realise,' he said, indicating his paper, 'that Arsenal only had six shots at goal?' So much, I thought, for possession football, which England so conspicuously fail to play. Out of the corner of my eye I saw the brim of David's trilby judder as he stopped a laugh. But we did affect amazement. It was after all our first serious introduction to match statistics.

Then Winterbottom left us, very cheerfully. I never saw him again – except, of course, on television.

Easter

Even after that defeat there was hope, and another run of victories. On Good Friday Portsmouth were beaten 6–1 at Old Trafford, and next day we went in the bus to Burnley. It was sunny and the pitch was dry but not too bouncy. United were beaten 4–2, after having had ample opportunities to win. At one blow Wolverhampton were emotionally out of reach, and everyone knew it. The mood on the bus was subdued. The way home passed the end of Moor Lane, Kersal, where I lived, and I asked Matt if I could be dropped off. When we were near I went down to the front and sat opposite him. He was half slumped and lost in his thoughts.

'Disappointing,' I said.

'Aye,' he said, and looked as vulnerable as I ever saw

him, except for a split second in our conversation about my articles, when he had realised my tack. I smiled and touched his brown Crombie sleeve. He recovered himself and asked Ted the driver to stop for me.

Next day we travelled to Portsmouth for the Easter Monday return. When David and I arrived at Old Trafford for the bus, there was Bill Foulkes.

'My old pal!' we said, delighted. 'Are you in?'

'Centre half,' he said, with a suppressed little grin that matched ours.

It was the first of the many games he played in that position, although he was not settled in it for another eighteen months. That day he blotted the strong, thoughtful Portsmouth centre forward Ron Saunders out of the match; which was won, and so was the next against Bolton Wanderers. Then it was away to Luton Town.

We stayed overnight in London and were taken by a local coach to Luton. Charlton was absent on international duty and in wet weather the game was a bad-tempered goalless draw. Then the bus took us to join the train at Watford. At one point Matt jerked his head for me to join him at the front.

'The driver's drunk,' he said. 'We'll never use this company again.'

Anything I can do for you

There was a meaningless home win against Birmingham City and then the last game of the season at Leicester. United were to go from there to London, and then by air to Rotterdam, to play a friendly against Feyenoord. It was to be their first flight since Munich. To prepare for it Matt and Louis Edwards had gone a few weeks earlier to Manchester Airport, had a few whiskies and booked themselves on a plane. I had given in my notice and would leave the paper after the match. Jack Smith had been persuaded, perhaps by the editor, to try out a newcomer for my job, and the idea was that we would go to Leicester together but that the newcomer would do the match report and go on to Holland. My wife and a friend would pick me up from Leicester railway station, and we would drive to London, where I hoped to be taken on by a literary agent. The newcomer, alas, was not prepossessing. He was smallish and nervous and I don't remember his name. No one, from Arthur Walmsley to Albert Scanlon, thought he would fit the bill. They were right, and when the next season started Peter Slingsby was the *Evening Chronicle*'s travelling reporter.

It was odd, after several years of Saturdays in press boxes, to sit there with nothing to do. The match went to and fro in front of me like television that I watched

but did not see, except that as United went down to a
2–1 defeat on another of those unsettled, blustery days,
I realised how much of the season had been out of kilter:
the weather with the moods of the team, me with myself,
and Busby with what might have been.

Although United finished five points behind the champions Wolves they had squandered that many at least.
They scored 103 goals: this is the total achieved by the
Babes when they won their second Championship, and
more than any United team since. Charlton hit twenty-
nine, and Albert Scanlon sixteen from the left wing,
although his were also the most vital misses, at Norwich
and Burnley in particular. 'Albert adds something,' Jimmy
Murphy used to say, and he did, not least a glorious
uncertainty. After one away game in which he had simply
put the ball past the fullback and run him ragged I said,
'Why don't you do that every week?' Albert stared out
of the train window, bit his nails and said, 'I don't know.'

Yet the crying need all season had been for something
more in defence. They conceded sixty-six goals, and the
totals for the four following seasons would be eighty,
seventy-six, seventy-five and eighty-one. It is no surprise
perhaps that when one late spring afternoon a Welsh
freelance rang up to say that Busby had offered Swansea
£50,000 for the Welsh centre half Mel Charles, and we
had very few minutes until edition time, we did not
check but ran the story, only to see it denied the next
day. Curiously Matt was not at all ruffled by this. I suppose
that when rumours were exposed it gave the impression
that he was calm. Others might panic, but not him.

His frustration did erupt again, however, after the Youth
Cup Semi-Final at Blackburn. Rovers were a bigger and
heavier team than United, and had future internationals

in Keith Newton and Fred Pickering, who put himself about a bit. United included Johnny Giles and Nobby Stiles, and the match was physical. As we left the ground through the players' entrance one of the Blackburn staff made a remark. Matt and Jimmy checked, and Matt savagely abused the man, accusing him of having been in his own day a clogger who couldn't play at all. It was an unusual lapse but to no avail: Blackburn went on to win the Cup.

As the game at Leicester flickered in front of me I knew that my overwhelming impression of the United players I had come to know was one of decent, well-intentioned people. There was a family atmosphere, and even the scrapes of the pre-Munich paradise had been innocent. When Roger Byrne crashed his car into the gatepost of Busby's neighbour, of all people, it was comical. When they covered Fred Goodwin's new car with snow, or stole his huge size-thirteen boots, it was schoolboyish. The ballrooms and coffee bars they went to had yet to see a lavatory drug deal, and the Cromford Club was a bastion of comic respectability. When the players stayed out late and found Jimmy Murphy awaiting them in their digs it was hardly a three-in-a-bed tabloid sensation, and the examplar of a Manchester United player was John Aston senior, who after Charlie Mitten went to Bogotá gave up his career as an England fullback to be Busby's emergency centre forward.

Crowther, Taylor and Quixall came from clubs with other cultures: more in tune with the average world of football, perhaps, but different and less idealistic, less interested in the wholesomeness of a person's character. United were in tune with a dream. If they were a family the players were the children, and they had accepted grown-up authority because it worked. Now, suddenly, success seemed far away again and there were the beginnings of puzzlement.

It was the same around Jack Smith's sports table. He had created an atmosphere that we were lucky to have known, but he had been helped by the events his men reported. At rugby league Great Britain had beaten Australia. Lancashire cricket had Brian Statham in his prime. Big stars like the miler Derek Ibbotson ran in Jack's athletics meetings, northern horses won the Grand National; and in soccer, the prime energy of it all, United and City had appeared between them in four successive Cup Finals, won the League twice, reached the Semi-Final of the European Cup twice, and played extraordinary attacking football. Now brightness was beginning to fade. At Maine Road Les McDowall's luck had begun to turn as his frustration with the board increased, and at Old Trafford it was clear that recovery would be slow; and the *Evening Chronicle* itself had run out of steam in its circulation war with the *News*.

As for myself, I never had a true reporter's temperament in the first place, and I had begun to make mistakes. At the end of the previous season I had felt elation, but now I sensed failure and unease. It was more than time for me to go.

All I remember of the farewells at Leicester railway station is that David and the players and Jack Crompton hurried through the barrier and down to the platform and that Matt and I were left alone. I was aware of a contrast between the tired bricks and metal and our emotions. For a moment we did not know what to do, and then Matt embraced me and said, 'I'm sorry you're leaving us, son. If there's anything I can do for you, let me know.'

'I will,' I said.

He turned and the ticket collector waved him through. Even at the time a voice said that I should have asked him for a pair of season tickets, but the fact is that I never asked for anything, except the okay to wear the club tie that Matt gave me. Perhaps that's why Jimmy sent me so many tickets later on. The tie I still have, as good as new, unworn because I was never convinced about the colour.

PART EIGHT
Prospero's Island

Seaside rep

When I left the paper my wife wanted to move to London, where it would be easier for her acting career, but I did not, yet, and was not sure that I could earn enough from television to meet our rising expectations. Then she was offered work for the summer with a seaside rep company at Llandudno, where we had a very amusing time and took our cat. In the autumn we looked for places in London, but they were too expensive and after that pregnancy and parenthood hit us like the tornadoes they are, and learning to write scripts was slow. I mean both the getting to know people by whom one would like to be known, and the writing itself: not the art, which is a gift, really, and present or not, but the mechanical part of it – the daily routine and the deadlines, and the struggle within oneself to come up with ideas. A few hundred words about a soccer match are not the same as a fifty-five-minute script that must be structured around commercial breaks.

When I had progressed a bit I met the director Michael Powell and sold him an idea for a film, so we took what money we had saved and spent six months on a Greek island hardly touched by tourism. Michael, in the cruel decline of his career, could never raise the money for the film, but I was in touch with him for years, and by one of those twists of life my second wife became one of his agents and attended his funeral, at which the address was given by Martin Scorsese. At the time I was in Peru, researching another show that never got made.

Back in 1950s Manchester my wife landed some jobs but mostly we were together, happy or at odds, with two of our eventual three children and not knowing that I was about to be given my first real breakthrough by *Z-Cars*. For three years there was little time or energy for football. I was fatalistic. United would recover or not. I followed them in the papers but attended hardly any matches: one of them gave me a last sight of Albert Scanlon, beating his man every time but crossing the ball into the side netting, and another a first of Denis Law playing for City. He sliced through the United defence in an abandoned derby at Maine Road. Then out of the blue, as Alf Clarke might have written, came a complete change.

The sports table lunch

In the intervening years Kemsley had sold its unwieldy empire to the Canadian entrepreneur Roy Thomson, a rationalising manager who soon called a halt to competition in Manchester, and set up a company with the *Guardian* and *Evening News* to own the *Evening Chronicle* together. The logic of this led to the *Chronicle* being closed down, which it was without warning in June 1962.

A day or two later I was telephoned by Don Frame, who said that the sports table was holding a farewell lunch at the Cromford Club, and would I like to go? I would and did. It was the first time I had seen some of them for a year or two, and would be the last that I ever saw of the majority.

A nightclub was an odd place to have lunch, with the tables pushed together to make a U shape on the dance floor, and here and there cracks of daylight that were brighter than the downlighters, but an air of dislocation suited the event. 'How are you, my old pal?' cried Jimmy, and Matt patted me on the back. There was a seating plan, and it placed me between them, with Arthur Walmsley next to Jimmy and Jack Smith to Matt.

The old spirit burned bright even if people had lost their jobs. Arthur was the name writer among them, and despite indifferent health wrote columns for the *Mirror* before he retired, to keep a post office on the Lancashire coast. Peter Slingsby had excellent shorthand and became a court reporter. The others found lesser subbing jobs on other papers. Their memorial is that when the *Evening News* got rid of them, it gave up its Saturday green final in favour of one printed on our own more famous pink paper, a remembrance to this day of Jack Smith, and of Alf Clarke's fractured prose.

Matt proposed the toast to the dead paper, and said that a bad thing had happened, but that we must hope that it led to something good. Jimmy assured Arthur and me that the *Chronicle* had always been their favoured paper, a sentiment he expressed in terms of which he rang first with the team news. Both the *Chronicle* and the *News* had been on the old Blackfriars exchange. But, as Jimmy said, 'It was always one two three four before two three four five.'

'Absolutely, my old pal,' said Arthur, and we had another drink on it.

For me, good did come out of this bad thing: my friendship with Jimmy picked up as though nothing had intervened except maybe a scouting trip or a close-season break. For the next five years, until we moved to London, he would send me tickets, and when he did not I stood at the Stretford End corner. Every couple of months or so one of us would phone the other and I would go down to the ground for a natter, sometimes after an evening game, and always for half a day in a close season. If I got good reviews for a play or was featured in some publicity, he would write a card that said 'Good show!' Once or twice he sent holiday postcards. 'SMACK ON THE IRISH SEA' said one from Colwyn Bay. When we talked it would as often as not be about show business, or people we knew and what had happened to them. Albert Finney, he thought, would look smarter if he wore a tie. Occasionally we would join Matt in his office for coffee, but more often it was the cubbyhole off the old board-room for something stronger. Jimmy did not tell me secrets any more, but he did regale me with an awful lot of football wisdom.

How many legs has he got?

Jimmy's conversational style was repetitive, with many paranoid glances behind him to see who was lurking, but it was never boring: topics resurfaced because events had cast new light upon them, and stories against himself contained cautionary paradoxes. 'I went to Barnsley to watch Tommy Taylor and I thought, I hope to Christ he has a bad game with all these other scouts here.' Later he took Matt to watch Taylor. They stood on the terraces and wore flat caps and dark glasses, and fondly imagined that they had not drawn attention to themselves.

Jimmy would cast Matt as a grand villain but had too much respect to invite people to laugh at him. The exceptions to this were the Barnsley outing to see Taylor and a story about a team talk. Matt would go through the team, explaining each person's duties, from goalkeeper to outside left, but when he came at last to Albert Scanlon there was no response.

'Albert?'

Nothing.

'Albert?'

No one there.

'Where is he?'

He was on the lavatory, with a cigarette and a Hollywood comic.

Jimmy's own team talks contained many a serio-comic gem, most famously the one before a teenage Wilf McGuinness was due to mark the mighty John Charles in a reserve game.

'How many legs has he got?'

'Two, Jim.'

'How many arms has he got?'

'Two, Jim.'

'Well then. He's a man like you are.'

Wilf, of course, was an adroit comedian's foil, and Shay Brennan was surely coming the blarney just a little when he protested that he did not want to stop his man unfairly. Jim rose to this with great effect: 'You don't have to kick him. Just leave your foot there.'

Other exhortations encapsulated in one sentence a profound philosophy of football.

'When you've got the ball you should never lose it, and when you do lose it you pick up the nearest opposing player.'

'When the winger has the ball the centre forward runs wide and the winger gives him the ball and runs ahead for the return.'

'A great team is when the ten players without the ball know what the man in possession is going to do.'

'Don't play the occasion. Play the match.'

Some saws were about football as an entertainment.

'A good referee is when you leave the ground and say "Who was the referee?"'

Opinions of players invariably implied a point beyond the particular.

'Finney was better than Matthews because Finney could do the lot.'

'It's a great pity that Francis Lee wasn't an inch taller.'

He would praise a touch of nastiness in a player, as when he recalled how on one of his first days as a United junior Dennis Viollet had kicked him in a practice match. But the only player with a truly difficult temperament that I heard him extol was Trevor Ford, of Swansea and Sunderland, a dark, brooding, unreliable but deadly centre forward with whom he had worked as Welsh manager.

And, of course, he would talk about the dark side of football – its callousness and its insecurity as a career. 'You must do your job properly,' he would say and fall silent, and fidget with his spoon or cigarette lighter. And out of the little brooding would come the flicked glance and the thought that worried him, which came bitterly true at the end of his own career. 'There's no room in football for nice men.'

A kid named Law

Jimmy's chatter apart, which many people thought eccentric, there was never much discussion at United, in offices, dressing rooms or on the bus, about players from other clubs, because not many of them were thought to be better than our men. Di Stéfano would be talked about, and Matthews and Finney, and sometimes John Charles, and Bill Foulkes admired the Bilbao centre half; and there was a kid at Huddersfield named Law. Busby had offered £10,000 for him after he played against United in the Youth Cup, but the Huddersfield manager Andy

Beattie would not sell. In 1960, however, Bill Shankly was in charge and he did sell Law, to Manchester City, and a year later City sold him to Torino: they made a profit of £55,000, but history would have been different if they had kept him. Law hated Italy and wanted to come back, and if there was a jaunty air about Matt and Jimmy at the sports table lunch, which there was, it must have been because they knew that they were about to get their man at last. Their journey to that point had been through the worst years of Busby's management.

The atmosphere at Old Trafford in the early 1960s has been well described in books by Eamon Dunphy and George Best. As Busby struggled to find a new way, staff morale deteriorated on and off the field. Like actors, footballers believe that they can do everything on their own but at the same time want sensible advice and discipline. At Old Trafford there seemed to be neither. Busby was distant, and at a time when tactical theories were becoming fashionable all he said was 'Go out and express yourselves' or 'Give the ball to a red shirt.' Training seemed boring: exercises without the ball, and the famous free-for-all car-park kickabout behind the Stretford End. There were cliques, rivalries, discontented mutterings and team meetings which purported to clear the air. Football echoed with rumours of match-fixing, which culminated in the prosecution of three Sheffield Wednesday players in 1963, and United were not untouched. But there was no evidence and Busby kept the club out of the papers.

From Matt's own point of view, as he recovered his personal equilibrium, he tried to carry on as normal. The club's share of insurance payments and damages from the Munich crash amounted to some £100,000 over five years. Even if Busby had wanted to buy a team he could not afford to, and youth players were given extended runs. When Wilf McGuinness broke his leg Maurice Setters was bought to replace him, and fullback Noel Cantwell's arrival from West Ham enabled Foulkes to settle at centre half. But other players were sold, and the arrival of Arsenal's centre forward David Herd was more than paid for by the departures of Dennis Viollet, for whom perhaps Busby's charisma had ceased to work, and Alec Dawson, whose development had been spoiled because he had to play too much after Munich.

In March 1962 United battled to the Cup Semi-Final, the first of five successive appearances, but they were well beaten by Tottenham, and in the League they finished fifteenth. Busby kept the European dream alive with friendlies against Benfica and Real Madrid, against whom I saw David Herd score a splendid solo goal, but Matt knew by now that there were not yet enough top-class youth players and that he would have to buy. Harold Hardman was still against it.

In my last reporting season David and I had always been aware of the turmoil around the United board-room as would-be directors jockeyed for position. Alan Gibson's friend Bill Young, a pleasant, mild, weak man was one, and Louis Edwards's brother-in-law Denzil Haroun another. Haroun was a smooth and affable representative of a type that even then had almost vanished but in the nineteenth century had given Manchester so much of its character: the textile merchant whose origins were foreign. The most famous of them, Friedrich Engels, was among the Germans whose subscriptions started the Hallé Orchestra, and his books and political views have influenced the entire world. Some, like the Greek Ralli brothers, became merchant princes. Another was the

father of the writer Elias Canetti. The Harouns had been
Syrian, and Denzil had the aquiline looks that would
have gone well with white samite and a scimitar through
his belt. I always liked him, and he would chat to David
and me in an earnest sort of way, as though he would
like to be one of the lads but on consideration preferred
life as it was. Harold Hardman's candidate was Gordon
Gibson, no relation of Alan but a headmaster and former
international referee. He was tall, bald, honest and
convinced that he knew what was right. He would give
Busby his forthright opinion of the game we had just
seen, and receive in return the most sympathetic of cold
shoulders.

Bill Young, of course, was the one to be elected, to
appease Alan Gibson, and in 1961 he joined Gibson and
Louis Edwards on a financial subcommittee, an important step towards the isolation of Hardman and the freeing
up of transfer money. More important in the long run
was the foundation in the same year of the Manchester
United Development Association.

For years Busby had dreamed of a stadium like the
ones he had seen in Europe, and in the rebuilding of
the Warwickshire County Cricket Club ground at
Edgbaston either he or Edwards saw the way. What
Warwickshire had done was run a football pool, and
United won permission from the FA to do the same.
Harold Hardman, a Methodist opposed to gambling,
disapproved, but Louis Edwards is supposed to have said
that he would take the responsibility. What this meant
I have often wondered. A meeting with God would
surely have run to Krug rather than the usual Edwards
fizz Dom Perignon; on the other hand it was probably
a dismissive reference to the likelihood of hellfire. We

never think that there will be regrets, do we, when we are sure of our purpose? So they poached Warwickshire's assistant development officer Bill Burke and made him secretary of the development association, which was a legally separate organisation from Manchester United and very soon a huge success. By 1965 it had paid for the new cantilever stand, in which Burke incorporated an idea from the now-defunct Manchester Racecourse: executive boxes. Burke was a visionary who understood the importance of all-year usage and cash flow. The catering facilities, the executive suites, the souvenirs and other ancillaries that are such a part of modern foot-ball were all begun by him at Old Trafford.

So it was that in the summer of 1962, when Law ran away from Italy, and Torino, piqued, tried to sell his contract to Juventus, Busby had the wherewithal to secure him. After a nervy month Torino accepted because they needed United's £115,000 fee. Busby had displayed the gambler's calm, and made his most important signing. Law was the most effective player I saw in a United shirt, and the greatest goal-front finisher of my time. Like Kenny Dalglish, he scored thirty goals for Scotland, but in half as many games, and whereas Jimmy Greaves would always score more against average teams, Law would nick one from the best, and that was the difference. He was hacked, tripped, elbowed and provoked in every game he played, and as Jimmy Murphy said to me, 'If the referees protected him he'd score fifty goals a season.' He was in addition an excellent all-round schemer, and when we see the cele-brated television clip of Scotland's Jimmy Baxter mocking England with his ball-juggle we should notice also that he is standing in space because Law has pulled every defender away and then back-heeled the ball to him. Baxter was the show-off, not the one they were afraid of.

Law's fee, nevertheless, put United into overdraft; and although his breathtaking speed made extraordinary things happen on the field that autumn, the rhythm still misfired and the team struggled against relegation. Busby knew that he needed more; he needed the board to go for broke, and I do not think it a coincidence that this was the moment at which Louis Edwards began to buy the shares that would make him the owner of Manchester United.

His life ambition

If we are to understand Big Louis's actions, and his eventual downfall, it is important not to use too much hindsight. In 1962 football clubs were not money-making assets for their directors. They offered prestige and business contacts to be sure, but directors were not allowed to receive fees, and dividends, of which there were not many, were capped at 5 per cent. Manchester United was a private company with 4,000-odd ordinary £1 shares, and just over 1,700 preference shares with limited voting power. Sales of shares had to be approved by the board, and if anyone did want to sell they would offer their stock to the board, who would buy at the £1 face value.

When Louis Edwards was made a director in 1958 the board sold him ten shares to comply with FA regulations, and up to 1961 he added seven more. There were 142 shareholders in all, of whom eight held more than a hundred units. Alan Gibson and his mother had 1,726 between them, some 41.8 per cent of the total, and Mabel Whittaker, the widow of George, had 468. But at that time, and indeed for years after Louis Edwards bought them, United shares were not financial assets like a quoted share on the stock market. There were not enough of them; there was no free market; and although they could be sold to someone who wanted a share of a football club, that was not in 1962 a profitable proposition. The value, in other words, was social and sentimental, which Louis Edwards had decided that he could afford to be, because he was on a high.

He and his brother Douglas had inherited the family meat company in 1943, since when they had developed it to a point where they had eighty retail outlets, contracts with Woolworths, Littlewoods and local authorities in Manchester, Salford and Lancashire, and a turnover of five million pounds. In 1962 they went public, and Louis had the cash to make Busby's power dream a reality.

At first he used an intermediary, Frank Farrington, an alderman and Manchester councillor since 1927, who was on the committees with which Edwards and Sons negotiated meat contracts. Farrington was not a rich man. He lived in a council flat, but he was persuasive and had great behind-the-scenes power. And there was a sentimental involvement: as a boy he had helped clear glass and stones from the old, notoriously bad Manchester United pitch at Newton Heath.

I met him once, when as part of the tests for my National Union of Journalists certificate of competence I had to conduct an interview in front of an examiner. Farrington was the volunteer interviewee, and he slumped in his chair like a droll, eye-flicking, cautious but fascinating old spider. Flies caught in his web would have been convinced that it was all for the best. And then he would have eaten them.

Farrington began with the little people who owned shares by chance: a parent or grandparent who had bought a few when United was formed before 1914 or in James Gibson's efforts to raise cash after 1932. The alderman would knock on the door one evening, ingratiate himself, accept a cup of tea, reminisce and offer five pounds a share. It was a gift from the blue. A day or two later the lucky sellers would go round to the Edwards company offices in New Street, Miles Platting. They were given cash, and were happy to pay Farrington a 5 per cent commission. Later they would receive a parcel of meat.

In the next phase Louis dealt by post. Dozens of letters offered fifteen pounds per share. 'The welfare and continued progress and success of Manchester United are now my life ambition,' he wrote, and it was true, because Busby the magician had enchanted him. On 16 October the board agreed the first deals, with more in December. Significant among these was the sale by Mabel Whittaker, widow of the man who had vetoed Edwards: she was alone and living on a pension. Significant too that at the end of December Busby was allowed to pay Glasgow Celtic £56,000 for Pat Crerand. He was the midfield organiser, the playmaker, the crucial last piece in the jigsaw. Not that it made much difference at first.

Bad weather stopped football in January, and United's League form did not pick up. In March, however, they began a spirited Cup run.

In January 1963 the board approved more share transfers to Edwards, but with a proviso: there were to be no more transfers to Alan Gibson or Louis Edwards that would cause any change 'in the present balance of holdings'. Transfers to outside individuals would be allowed.

The response came in March, with letters to shareholders from Douglas Edwards and Denzil Haroun. 'May I introduce myself to you as a regular and ardent supporter of Manchester United . . . ?'

Hardman in hiding

Alan Gibson had lifelong bad health. He was a stubborn man who hated confrontation, and he had promised his dying father that he would always support Matt Busby. Bill Young was an engaging cipher, and Harold Hardman, the little stickler, was eighty-one years old. He owned a mere seventy-one shares in Manchester United and at one point offered to sell them to anyone who would stop Louis Edwards; but no one had the will to do so, or perhaps the inclination to oppose Matt Busby. It was at this point, in the spring of 1963, that Hardman did a very human, sad and extraordinary thing: he ran away.

I know this because Matt Busby told Arthur Walmsley, who told me, and to tell Arthur in the first place was a masterpiece of spin. He was sworn to confidence, but in such a way that if the story got out, which it did not, Arthur, who was trusted by everyone, would be around to defuse it. Who better than Arthur to confirm that the poor, admirable old man was confused and exhausted by having given his all? Harold had always been a no-nonsense person and now that glory re-beckoned he wobbled. Because United were in the Cup Final, thanks to Law's semi-final goal against Southampton, when he did not attempt to kick the ball but bent his knees and let it bounce off him into the net, a level of split-second improvisation that only the geniuses attain.

Hardman ran to London, where he stayed in a cheap hotel near Earls Court Square and on Saturdays walked the few hundred yards to watch Chelsea from the Stamford Bridge terraces. After three or four weeks Matt and Big Louis appeared in the hotel lobby, and the little man who had played outside left for Great Britain in the 1908 Olympics smiled and said, 'I always knew you'd find me.' My guess is that they simply asked his wife where he was, but they did not explain this to Arthur. Nor of course had they mentioned the rush to buy shares.

Over Easter United played their Cup Final opponents Leicester City twice, with football that was light years ahead of them but brought only one point. Jimmy told me afterwards that a bicycle kick Law crashed against the bar was one of the hardest shots he had ever seen. But they did escape relegation, and on the day, on the ballplayer's Wembley greensward, and with Harold Hardman safely in the Royal Box, they won the Cup 3–1 and the lost rhythm restored itself. Law scored another classic, running away from goal and abruptly wheeling, and Pat Crerand seemed to be the only man in possession of the ball. They were Manchester United again, and the dream was up and running.

So was the share buying, and two of the deals had echoes, had anyone known about them. Clarence Hilditch, player-manager for a year in the 1920s, sold his twenty shares, and Douglas Edwards had the grace to go himself to Winifred Meredith, daughter of the immortal Billy, to buy her sentimental holding of eight. In September 1963, by which time the price had risen to twenty-five pounds, Alan Gibson succumbed and agreed to part with the shares that would give Louis Edwards an absolute majority. The board waived its previous objections and the deal went through. Denzil Haroun was made a director, and in December 1964 Louis became vice chairman. In the summer of 1965 Harold Hardman died and Louis became chairman. He had paid something between £30,000 and £41,000. Gate receipts for the 1963/4 season were £172,000.

Louis had bought the power but it was Matt who deployed it. He bought and sold as he saw fit. He negotiated the players' contracts and drew up the directors' rota for attendance at Central League games. He took counsel's opinion on the Munich crash suit against British European Airways, and he made the perimeter advertising deals. He discussed with the FA and FIFA their proposals for World Cup games at Old Trafford, and every day he and Jimmy dreamed about the European Cup.

Without him we'd win nothing

Freewheeling attacking football had made Real Madrid and Benfica the champions of Europe, and Brazil of the world, but the tide was turning against it, a fact that was completely ignored by United's efforts to rebuild. When Busby and Murphy started they were revolutionaries, tracksuited figures who trained with the players. Elsewhere, everyone except Arsenal played the W formation, players were expected to have learned their trade, and men in suits picked them and sent them out to play. By the mid-60s Matt and Jimmy were the men in suits. Bill Nicholson had coached Spurs to the double, and his captain Danny Blanchflower had begun the obsession with rehearsed dead-ball plays. The West Ham academy managers had begun to appear in their tracksuits, Bill Shankly had promoted himself as an inspirational fanatic, and Ramsey had won the World Cup. It was a world of born-again tacticians in which it seems almost incredible that the best team in Europe, and one of the most thrilling in history, was run by two elderly men who had theories, put players together accordingly, and then more or less let them get on with it. But that is exactly what Busby and Murphy did to create their last and most extraordinary team.

Not, I think, that Busby was ever a great match

tactician. His idea in Madrid of marking di Stéfano with Eddie Colman in one half of the field and Jackie Blanchflower in the other was a blunder, and for a long time he does not seem to have been persuaded of the necessity for caution in European away legs. Busby recognised great players and great football, and he had the priceless knack of being able to deal with the highest and most creative talents. He could both inspire and discipline them, an instinct which deserted him only for a year or two in the early 1960s and at the very end of his hands-on career, when it is often forgotten that he was old enough to be George Best's grandfather: in other words, when there was a huge gap in experience and assumptions.

What Busby knew as a fundamental was that players are not equally talented, and that even the most talented will not get anywhere if their attitude is wrong. What he wanted were talented players who were also reliable human beings, which is why he preferred to develop people rather than to buy them. Murphy, who was a genius as a coach and an assessor of talent, and very clever tactically, was crucial to this idea. He picked the most talented people he could find, moulded them, and delivered them to the first team ready to play. They would not need a complicated tactical system because they had been encouraged in responses for all seasons. When they were in the first team Matt wanted them to express themselves, and knew when to pull a youngster out so that he learned without losing much confidence. Young and old, if they lost form they returned to the reserves, where Jimmy embarked upon remedial exhortations.

In the years immediately after Munich this system operated in theory, but in practice everyone's development had been disrupted, and Matt and Jimmy were more tired and remote. The teams led by Johnny Carey and Roger Byrne were managed in one way, the assembly that featured Law, Best and Charlton in another. In one sense the team was hardly managed at all. It was spun out of the air, from Jimmy's notions of how one sort of talent should complement another to create a rhythm, and from Matt's charisma, his ability to lift people above themselves and involve them in his dream. It is difficult to describe what they did, because it was improvisation and magic, and what George Best did cannot be taught. 'Leave him alone,' said Murphy to the others. 'Just leave him alone and let him play.' If there are lessons they are about psychological things, I suspect, and about the quest for balance, the underlying rhythm that when it is there is undeniable. And of course the glorious mundane things in Jimmy Murphy's world, like the way they would start at a high tempo to try to get an early goal, and the occasion on which I made a long and abstruse point and he said, 'Yes. You're right. But they should have attacked when they had the wind behind them.'

In statistical terms, between 1962 and 1968 they won the FA Cup once and were semi-finalists five times. They won the League twice, were runners-up twice and fourth once. They won the European Cup and were beaten in the semi-finals, and reached the final of the old Inter Cities Fairs Cup and the quarter-final of the Cup Winners' Cup. They introduced during these years another generation of youth players: there were four home-grown players in the team that beat Leicester City and eight in the European Cup Final.

Of their transfer dealings the most interesting sale

was that of Johnny Giles, who resented having to play on the wing and was unmoved by Busby's charm. He asked to go and he went, to become the playmaker of Leeds United. Of Busby's purchases, Stepney was the best goalkeeper United had until Schmeichel and John Connelly was an excellent right-winger who scored goals. The one failure was Graham Moore, a Welsh inside forward who faded after a brilliant debut. 'He wanted to play all that short stuff,' Jimmy told me, which means that in a dressing room full of genius Moore lost the confidence to give anything more than a safe and boring pass. In other days he might have been coached back, but in the arena of magic spells he was discarded. There was no time; and after they realised that they had another good generation of kids, who won the Youth Cup in 1964, Jimmy travelled more and more with the first team: advising, chatting, suggesting and generally attempting to hypnotise.

In the middle of it all, in March 1966, came the European Cup Quarter-Final against Benfica. Jimmy sent me a ticket for the first leg at Old Trafford and it was a tense battle of wits which United won 3–2. Nobby Stiles put on a masterly display of man-marking against Eusebio, which he was to repeat three months later in the World Cup Semi-Final, and it was this I suspect which undermined Benfica's confidence, because in the Lisbon return they were swept aside. United's 5–1 victory was the truest high-water mark of British football. It was mythic, and it made a world personality of George Best. Yet when I see the grey flickering television tape of the game I think as I did at the time that the true star was Denis Law, whose pace and passing split the Portuguese time after time.

'Without him,' confided Jimmy Murphy, who knew well the fragility of magic, 'we'd win nothing.'

The semi-final against Partizan Belgrade was a numbing disappointment. In the first leg Best and Connelly carried injuries and United were beaten 2–0. This was the match in which Best contrived to stand on the ball to avoid being hacked. The return at Old Trafford was listless. United won 1–0 but were out, to a team that was big and strong but nothing special.

It was in the close season after this match that Busby put Law on the transfer list. The maximum wage had been abolished in 1961 and United, for all that they had the biggest stars, were the lowest payers in the First Division. Other clubs had one or two stars, argued Busby, and could pay them high wages. It was because United had so many top players that they could not afford to pay them all top salaries. So when Law demanded more he put him on the list, made him sign a letter of apology and then because he'd apologised did a secret deal for half the rise he'd asked for. It was breathtaking man management, and yet a question remains.

That the magic team did not win more trophies is due to the fact that it was exhausted by injuries, replays and fixture pile-ups. One became as sick of the sight of cloggers and desperate self-sacrificing runners as one is today of teams with eight men across the edge of their penalty area. The Babes had been a conscious use of the squad system. Why did Matt not realise that to apply the system in a changed world clubs would have to keep a lot of players on high wages, as they do today? Or perhaps he did realise but simply could not bring himself to do it. Personally he was curiously uninterested in money, as gamblers are not, of course: what matters is the experience.

How to referee a grudge match

Through Matt's good offices Arthur Walmsley was made FIFA press liaison officer for the 1966 World Cup games at Old Trafford. The teams in the group were Brazil, Portugal, Hungary and Bulgaria, but Brazil played all their games in Liverpool, at Goodison Park, and the Manchester public's response was lukewarm. The highest attendance was just under 30,000 for the game between Portugal and Hungary, which was ruined by a first-minute injury to the Hungarian goalkeeper. Portugal won 3–1. Half their team were from Benfica, and we reckoned we had already seen them off. But drinks in the press centre were fun and Arthur was in his element: years later David Meek did the equivalent job at the European Championships.

The only game I travelled to see was the Goodison Park semi-final between Russia and West Germany. My wife, our friend Herbert Wise and I decided that we would like to go, drove to Liverpool and bought some tickets. We stood among garrulous Liverpool dockers. When I saw the 1998 semi-final in Marseilles my son had bought the tickets two months earlier from the New York office of French Railways at a ludicrously surcharged price, and we sat with Americans, Africans and Japanese. These last were supporting Brazil and carried rising sun banners on which was written GO BRAZIL! NIPPON WITH YOU!

The referee at Goodison, where the Germans beat Russia 2–1, one of the goals being a piledriver from Franz Beckenbauer, was the elegantly moustached Italian Lo Bello, and he showed excellent sense and urbanity by holding himself to one side while the two teams, who had not met since the war, solemnly kicked lumps out of each other in the dirtiest big game I ever saw. How wise Lo Bello was. The better team won, and if he had tried to impose the rules there could only have been fisticuffs.

Years later, when I was working as Franco Zeffirelli's rewrite man on his television epic *Jesus of Nazareth*, our producer was an Italian with a similar name, La Bella, and he was every bit as sophisticated and adept at avoiding trouble as his near namesake. Goodison Park I did not see again until November 1998, when Ferguson's United gave a beautiful display of football to feet in thrashing Everton 4–1.

England won that 1966 World Cup, of course, which to my mind was as big a disaster as it was a triumph.

Wingless wonders

It was inevitable, after the great attacking teams of the 1950s, that football coaches would seek defensive parity. As so often, the Milan clubs were in the van. The Spaniard Helenio Herrera created at Inter Milan as solid a defend and counter-attack team as there has ever been, and re-inforced a defensive-minded club culture that persists to this day. In the mid-60s they won a brace of Italian titles, European Cups and World Club Championships. AC Milan won the European Cup twice and the Cup Winners' Cup once. Juventus won three national titles but failed in Europe, probably because their tradition has always inclined more to attack. Defensive Argentinian teams won the South American Cup ten times between 1964 and 1975, and in the World Cup Alf Ramsey's guerrilla victory at Wembley confirmed the trend, and gave it a particularly English athletic twist. Although Jack Charlton was a marker and first-time clearer of the ball, both Ramsey's fullbacks were at ease on it, Stiles was very good and Bobby Moore was brilliant. Unfortunately this solidity and skill at the back was not what English club football and the press seized upon. What they seized upon was that he seemed to have discarded wingers and ballplay up front in favour of hard work.

In his contempt for publicity and laypeople Ramsey himself neither discussed nor elucidated his decisions, but what he did was to express in terms of team selec-tion a sensible football habit. When teams attack they try to make the pitch as wide as possible, and when they defend they try to make it narrow. Everybody does it, every weekend. What Ramsey did was to select a narrow team with tucked-in midfielders instead of wingers. It was a smart use of his resources and made it very diffi-cult for better teams to create.

Geoff Hurst was Ramsey's target man but ran here and there all the time. The other forwards ran people ragged in midfield, and stopped their progress. Bobby Charlton was the genius fetch-and-carry, and it was

England's luck perhaps that he scored vital individual goals. It was percentages stuff, waiting for gaps to appear late on, and corners. But playing at home it worked.

Jimmy Murphy predicted it but I had not believed him. In the autumn I saw him again and said that I should have known better. He shook his head and said that he was afraid Alf Ramsey would now go on to failure.

'He had elocution lessons,' he said.

'What?' I said.

'He thinks he knows how to speak.'

Jimmy's own voice was an unmistakeable, rapid, cigarette-gravelled, slightly amazed Welsh lilt.

'How d'you mean?' I said.

'Now he thinks he knows how to play football.'

It was a cruel comment but not without resonance. In their Championship season Ramsey's half-narrow Ipswich had been thrashed 5–0 at Old Trafford, the system rumbled and the ballplayers let loose against it, while Busby and Murphy still sought the underlying mystery, the hidden rhythm, as the sculptor seeks the statue in the stone. They were idealists who had a dream and then looked for the players to express it. Ramsey was a pragmatist who invented systems to fit the players. His tragedy, which I think Murphy foresaw, was that he failed to come up with anything new, was too loyal to players past their best, and at the 1970 World Cup was outthought at his own game of guerrilla warfare.

In their 1970 defeat by Brazil England were again on top in the last quarter when Ramsey brought on the West Bromwich centre forward Astle, who did not have the skill to get through. What if he had used instead the far classier Alan Clarke? What if in the quarter-final he had picked Stepney to keep goal instead of Bonetti? Bonetti tended to stay on his line but, like the injured Banks, Stepney came out. Would he have challenged for the crosses that gave Germany their goals? And, crucially, what if Ramsey had pulled off his exhausted left back Cooper? Would the German substitute winger Grabowski have turned the game nonetheless?

Impossible to know, and Ramsey himself maintained his awkward inscrutability. His Ipswich and England triumphs will stand, however, like ancient monuments in a cheaper landscape.

Consequences

If the 1966 World Cup made football sexy in England and attracted a middle-class public that had not been there before, it also showed how tolerant referees had become of rough play. That of course was an essential ingredient of the new defensive dispensation. The slide tackle and the tackle from behind were not illegal, and defenders who were quicker than those of former years could deliver them when they were beaten or when they wanted to play the man and not the ball. Italian defenders it is true had always liked to stay on their feet, but to do so they developed the arts of the body-check, the shirt tug and the nudge to unbalance a jumping man, to which the Argentinians added the gob of spit in the hair or face. The Germany–Russia Semi-Final may have been an understandable replay of the Battle of Stalingrad, but for many other games in that 1966 World Cup there was no such excuse.

Pelé, the world's outstanding player, was hacked down in Brazil's first match, rested in their second to allow his cuts and bruises to heal, and in the third so viciously fouled by his Portuguese marker that he became a helpless passenger on the wing. Both Uruguay and Argentina were involved in unpleasantness in their games against West Germany, whose inside forward Helmut Haller began in this tournament that German trick of the exaggerated roll upon the ground when fouled. Nobby Stiles was protected by his manager after a wrecking tackle upon the Frenchman Simon, whereas the Argentinian captain Rattin was sent off against England for arguing with the German referee.

The conviction among South Americans that Pelé should have been protected and his assailants sent off, and that Uruguay and Argentina had been the victims of refereeing decisions that favoured England and West Germany led to a deterioration in relations between the continents. The World Club Championship became the battleground on which Argentinian teams took their revenge against Europe, and in FIFA itself there was a change in the balance of power. The Brazilian Havelange saw his opportunity. In his opinion Europe's attitude was one of contempt for the rest of the world, and by promising more places in the finals of an enlarged World Cup he gradually enlisted the votes of FIFA's African and Asian members, so that in 1974 he was elected president in place of England's Sir Stanley Rous. What FIFA did during the next twenty-four years is controversial, and there have been many accusations: that Ronaldo's bizarre contribution to the 1998 World Cup Final, for example, was about advertising contracts and not football sense. But for good and ill Havelange shaped world football, and he could not have held on to his support for so long without the events of 1966.

Prime Minister Harold Wilson may have appeared on the balcony of the England team's hotel, and London may have swung, but as well as its consequences for FIFA the World Cup granted extended licences to some of the deepest bad habits of English football. Aren't ballplayers always selfish and unreliable? Let's get Brazil on one of our February mudheaps, and then see how good they are. What you want to look for is lads who get stuck in, make themselves available, put themselves about, run their bollocks off and generally accept that it's a man's game. This, rather than a bit of smart thinking about the game, is what Ramsey's victory was perceived to have vindicated. Work rate was the mantra and its echo was long. Brian Clough was a good advocate, Liverpool the most successful team: a star striker, a cruel ball-winner, an outside left as the outball and a half-narrow midfield packed with Scots and Irish – a brilliant percentages team. But when in 1994 FIFA outlawed the tackle from behind the ball-winners knew that they never would walk alone, because there was a man with a yellow card at their side. That as much as television money was the end of an era, and United, with their unceasing emphasis on skill, profited more than most.

Bicycle chains

Beneath the supposed good times of the 1960s something was going wrong, of course, and a change in the behaviour of football crowds was an early warning. The first serious violence I saw was at Old Trafford when at the Stretford End Everton supporters whirling bicycle chains attempted to capture the United banners. I date this event to August 1966, because the banners had been banned for a good eighteen months before they were unfurled at Wembley for the 1968 European Cup Final. The educational and social impoverishment that bred this violence, the slow collapse of the old industrial society, the realisation by frustrated young men bombarded with consumer advertising that the depicted good life was out of reach, and their tribal adherence to football teams as the only drama that gave life resonance and a sense of history were no doubt what Harold Wilson should have worried about instead of rushing into photo opportunities with the Jules Rimet Trophy. United fans were made particularly destructive, I suppose, by the very fact that the dream was so pervasive and the football so brilliant.

But generally thuggishness off the field did nothing to discourage thuggishness on it, and vice versa.

The fact that the old working class was losing the

sense of its place in the world is in my opinion as respon-
sible as the hard-running game for the failure of so many
major English football talents to develop. Alan Hudson,
the most gifted schemer of the 1970s, played twice for
England and frittered away his career. His Chelsea team-
mate Osgood played four times, Charlie George once,
Stan Bowles four and Rodney Marsh nine. Tony Currie
played seventeen times. Talented and very fit young men
will always be exuberant, but to look at this generation
of names is to see wastage on a positively social scale.
One of the reasons why so many of the playmakers at
English clubs were Scots or Irish is that they were
educated to believe that they could progress with dignity.
English society has long been snobbish, and the ruinous
excesses of a Paul Gascoigne are as much to do with
embarrassment and a sense of inferiority as with temperament. David Platt and Gary Lineker, on the other hand,
were in the 80s as indicative of a generation as comfortable with its fame and wealth as Roger Byrne might
have been had he lived.

Some football cultures were helped by the mood after
1966. The German panzers rolled to one triumph after
another because they were skilled as well as ruthless and
methodical, and the successes of Argentinian clubs were
to be the platform for their performances in the World
Cup. And in Holland something new emerged: the
counter to the relentless defensive pressure: so-called total
football.

Total football, as practised by Ajax of Amsterdam and
the Dutch national team, blurred the distinction between
attackers and defenders, and a normal sense of positions
on the field. If a winger went back to defend, and his
fullback broke ahead of him, they would stay where they

were until a new situation allowed them to reposition themselves in a natural way. Forwards had to cover and tackle, defenders to take men on. It was difficult to mark or to track the Dutch, and because everything was fluid the opposition's shape was pulled this way and that.

'We attack together and we defend together,' Jimmy Murphy told his young players in the 50s, and there was a great deal of total football in the way the Babes played, particularly when the skilful Jackie Blanchflower was at centre half.

Ajax were in three European Cup Finals in the 1970s, winning twice, and Holland in two World Cup Finals. At club level they suffered because the players went elsewhere for higher wages, but the legacy of this epoch in Dutch football was the Will Coerver system of coaching children, which has produced a steady flow of talent and contributed to another excellent Ajax team in the 90s.

In the England of the 1970s and 80s the consequence of Ramsey's victory was that power prevailed. Ballplaying teams sometimes won the Cup but hard running and defending dominated the League and even the European Cup, which English clubs won seven times with percentages teams in which the creatives were usually Irish or Scots. In the World Cup England reached the quarter-finals in 1970, failed to qualify in 1974 and 1978, and qualified but were knocked out at the group stage in 1982. Results in the European Championships were no better, and it is difficult to resist the conclusion that whatever the managers did there was neither sophistication nor quality in depth in our football. Then at the European Cup Final of 1984 Liverpool fans rioted, Juventus fans were killed, and English clubs were banned from Europe.

In the same year more than 250 people were killed or injured in a fire at Valley Parade, Bradford, and in 1989 ninety-five people died at Hillsborough. In its isolation English football was forced to look at itself, its violent supporters and its rickety stadiums. It is no coincidence, perhaps, that with the clubs out of Europe there was a more sensible focus on the national team, which in 1986 was thrust from the World Cup Quarter-Final by Maradona's Hand of God, and in 1990, under Bobby Robson's pragmatic, player-friendly regime, lost its semi-final on penalties. It could be argued here that Paul Gascoigne, famously weeping because he had been sent off for a ludicrous tackle, should have been hauled into the dressing room so that the team's focus became the shoot-out and not him. But perhaps that was the flip side of the way Robson handled his men.

By 1990 television money had begun to flow, and with the formation of the Premier League, a long overdue admission that standards could not rise if the big clubs were held back, it became a flood. The Taylor Report on the Hillsborough Disaster recommended all-seater stadiums and the government insisted, so that what Ted Coghill had typed up in Busby's articles – about elite teams performing in comfortable arenas – became some sort of a reality at last.

Would the minds of football people and politicians have been sharpened so quickly without the catastrophes? Almost certainly not. It was a tough way for everyone to learn, and the losers were Liverpool, who missed further opportunities in Europe, and whose supporters had been involved in two of the disasters.

European Cup

To look at United's Championship and 1968 European Cup-winning team against this historical background is to see that although it was masterful it was out of fashion. The tide was running against imaginative football, and in favour of Leeds and Liverpool. Consider here Shankly's three great maxims:

Never allow a forward to turn, and when he does hunt him down.
Never carry the ball out of your own penalty area.
Always back up the man with the ball.

This, it will be seen at once, is not a description of how to play quality football, but of how to defend against and destroy it. It is pragmatic but depressing, and the thinking behind it, the deliberate curbing of ambition to what is possible for people of average ability, tells us why Chapman's Arsenal, Rowe's Tottenham and United's own teams of 1948 and 1958 had no imitators. Most Britons have come to prefer mediocrity. It is easier to live with.

On the other hand, can wizards be imitated? Put this sort of wonderful player next to that one, said the book of spells, and the result will be magic. And abracadabra! It was.

Of course, Jimmy had written the book, and the team at its strongest exhibited many of his notions. The goal-keeper Stepney dominated his penalty area. Dunne was a fast and clever fullback, Noble a hard-hitting one. Crerand was a creative wing half who could tackle, Stiles a defender who could play. At centre half Bill Foulkes was a marker who made sensible little clearances to his creators. There was a similar balance of qualities going forward. Connelly or young John Aston were direct wingers and Best was a dribbler. At centre forward Herd was the target. Law was a striker who could scheme and Charlton a schemer who could strike, and two different attacking modes could be employed at any time: Crerand's sense of a passing movement and Charlton's of a through run. When these failed Best could shimmy through an entire defence on his own, or Law produce a goal from sheer athleticism. It is the quality of these two in partic-ular, I suppose, that gave the thing its extraordinary sense of improvisation, and of there being no end to the reper-toire. One could see that it was vulnerable, and at the same time that there would never again be anything quite like it in one's lifetime. And indeed, like that of 1948, the most deadly magic did only exist for one season, as injuries and transfers took their toll.

The following season Manchester City, that other club who believe in beautiful football, won the League with a more drilled attacking routine, but when they tried to jazz it up by signing Rodney Marsh they lost balance. The moral, I guess, is that the book of spells is decep-tive. Or that some wizards are more wizardy than others.

One evening in the autumn of 1967 I went to a game by a route that like earlier ones – like the trains or the office cars with Arthur Walmsley – had become a habit: on the Number 2 bus through Salford, and then by foot across crofts and along rows of back-to-backs. There was a hazard in the form of a swing bridge across the Ship Canal, and sometimes this would open and people be 'bridged', as the saying was. Then I hurried across railway lines, past Callender's Insulated Cables and a grain elevator, turned left into a denser crowd and as often as not took the back way, the little cobbled lane with the new stand on one side and a factory wall on the other, to a corner crush barrier or a seat that Jimmy had given me.

On this occasion I had arranged to have a drink with him, but with ten minutes to go I saw Joe Armstrong's little walk as he came along the alleyway. The seat next to mine was empty and he sat in it.

'He's busy,' he said. 'Called away. Can't see you. You know how it is.'

'Absolutely,' I said. 'I know how it is.'

'Good lad,' said Joe, and patted me on the hand.

He limped away past the shouting crowd, the folk-loric old fixer whose lies one forgave because there was no disdain in them.

Three months later we left Manchester to live in London, but there was time to see United beat Hibernian of Malta in the first round of the European Cup. The Hibernian manager was a priest and at one point he went onto the field in his cassock, to attend an injured player. The last League game I saw at Old Trafford, for many years as it turned out, was against Southampton, a very physical team in those days, and the crowd was angry.

That European campaign United played tighter football

in the away legs and their name was on the trophy from the first, really, even when they went behind in the second leg of the semi-final in Madrid. Things must have been bad because, according to Bobby Charlton, 'even Jimmy said nothing' at half-time. But with a miracle of the spirit they rallied, and appropriately enough it was Billy Foulkes who trundled upfield to score the goal that put them into the final against Benfica.

A couple of days before the match the *Guardian* asked me to write a preview piece, and I telephoned Jimmy at the team's hotel in Egham.

'Come over,' he said. 'You must see the bedroom. You'll love the four-poster.'

It was a Tudor mansion in a formal garden, and apart from the throbbing of a television generator-van the afternoon was quiet and drowsy. They had told Bill Foulkes and David I was coming, and we had a catch-up chat before Matt and Jimmy and I had a stroll in the garden and a coffee. The players were resting. The only one I saw was Alex Stepney. Jimmy took me to see the four-poster and gave me some tickets for the game. We didn't talk about anything in particular. I could see their concentration from the way in which they listened to Stepney: watching, waiting, assessing him, ready to settle a player and make him clear about his tasks. Then I drove home across London and wrote my article.

I described the hotel and the mood there, and rather than rehash a lot of sentimentalities about Munich I remembered an old man who had come into the *Evening Chronicle*'s offices once. He was in a bad way and needed cash so he thought he could sell his story. This was 'Knocker' West, one of the United players suspended for life in 1915 for fixing a match with Liverpool. Jack Smith thanked him and gave him a fiver from petty cash. I said that I hoped today's United played hard for him, as well as for the rest of us.

So they did, I guess, in an unfamiliar all-blue strip, on a warm evening when they carried the game to opponents who died hard. By 1968 Benfica were a declining force and United did not have the absolute quality of the previous encounter. But it was a good contest, between teams whose players liked and admired one another. The turning point came with some ten or twelve minutes to go and the score 1–1. Eusebio broke clear at last, but Stepney held his swerving piledriver. At the end of ninety minutes the players sprawled on the turf and Matt and Jimmy came out in their blazers. I thought how avuncular they looked, and how ten years before Jimmy would have seemed a wild man, somehow, but now he didn't. Whatever they said it kept their men on track. Best scored one of his street-football goals; Kidd and Charlton added another one each, and that was it. After twelve years they had won the European Cup.

I left before they paraded it, to get a quick start out of the car park. It was historic, and it was the end of something, and they would settle for it; but I knew enough to understand that it was not actually the dream. The dream was about domination and would have to go on.

PART NINE
Say it Ain't So

One of those things you don't do

At the end of Shakespeare's play *The Tempest* Prospero, who has ruled his island by cruelty and magic, forswears his spells and leaves the island to assume his rightful dukedom. But Matt's only dukedom was Old Trafford, the island of magic and the subordinated Louis Edwards, and one knew in one's heart that he would never leave it. Later, when he was very old, it was clear that he had been held by a need for money as well as everything else; at the time I just thought that he would never allow anyone the free hand that would enable them to continue his achievements. He would not be outdone, as Shankly was. The legend, I knew, must stand alone to be a legend.

In a stage play with a happy ending he would have gone as soon as they beat Benfica, no doubt, but in real life there was indecision. In the close season he was knighted and he bought the Burnley winger Willie Morgan for £105,000 when what was needed was a top defender. In January 1969 he announced that he would step down, and Jimmy Murphy with him, but not the name of his successor. In February a Gallup Poll voted him Britain's seventh most popular man. In March United lost the away leg of their European Cup Semi-Final against AC Milan and failed to make up the deficit at

Old Trafford, where the referee disallowed a perfectly good goal for offside, and the steam went out of the game after a half-brick thrown from the Stretford End hit the Italian goalkeeper's head. In April Busby said that he would become general manager and Wilf McGuinness, who was thirty-one and running the youth team, chief coach. I was not surprised. In one of our very first conversations after Munich Jimmy Murphy had said that in his opinion Wilf was manager material.

Jimmy was in limbo, waiting for the club to make a settlement, but he sent me tickets for the first game of the next season, which was at Crystal Palace. After the match Wilf waved at me through the coach window: he still looked like one of the lads. Their new London hotel was the Russell, and I went there several times that season. Once I had lunch with Matt, and I tried to persuade him to appear in a television documentary – not about his life but about the nature of football, which Granada was keen to do. But he never in his life gave a television interview outside a news item, except once years later about Scottish football, and he let me down gently. He allowed Granada to rush him so that he could refuse them, and not me to my face. Confrontation was not really his style. Later I rode for one last time on the team bus, from White Hart Lane to the Russell after a night match, and on another occasion I was on the fringe of a team talk Wilf gave.

After it Bobby Charlton came up with a piece of paper that Wilf had left on the table: it was the names he intended to field and a tactical jotting. 'Isn't this one of the things you don't do?' said Bobby's subversive grin. 'Leave clues for the opposition?'

They love Wilf, I thought, but they don't respect him, and it will end badly.

In his second season they drew the Cup Semi-Final against Leeds. The replay was floodlit. George Best spent the afternoon in bed with a woman he picked up in the hotel bar. Wilf burst into the room but did not drop him. George had a stinker and missed an open goal. The match was drawn but Leeds won the second replay. Just before Christmas 1970 Matt, who had the board in his pocket and had vetoed most of Wilf's transfer ideas, told him that he had been asked by the directors to take over the team again, and the agonising years began.

How did they get on?

A few weeks before Wilf was sacked my own career took its decisive turn. The director Bill Bryden was assigned to my play *Pirates* at the Royal Court Theatre. He is an original and dynamic Scotsman from Greenock (his school team contained the future Chelsea ball-juggler Charlie Cooke), and his opening words to me were 'What this play needs is high-energy ball-winners in the middle of the park,' a conflation of football and theatre that for the next fifteen years confused many but made perfect sense to us. We did nine plays together, four of them at the National Theatre, where the ball-winners who figured in *Pirates* became his famous acting company. Bill absorbed me and I him: he was Busby, I suppose, and I was Murphy, but between me and the real United there was now a distance, because I did not know Frank

O'Farrell. He was a Catholic of high principles who had been a player at West Ham, where he had sat in on the famous academy. What the academy taught I have never been entirely sure, and I think that it was Dennis Viollet who said to me, 'If it's an academy how come I get kicked there more than anywhere else?' Unfair no doubt, and to judge from the teams coached by its alumni Malcolm Allison, Dave Sexton, Ken Brown and O'Farrell it tried to reconcile the new snuffing-out with as much ballplay as possible. O'Farrell himself had done well at Torquay and Leicester, and what Busby liked was his toughness in dealing with players, which as the legends declined and discipline strayed, would now be required at Old Trafford.

In fact O'Farrell was third choice after Jock Stein of Celtic and Dave Sexton of Chelsea, both of whom turned United down. He had some early success both on and off the field. He persuaded Busby to move out of his big office, and he told the board that it would cost a million to rebuild the team. In the event he spent half that, but of his new players only Martin Buchan was a true success and one, Ted McDougall, was simply not a Manchester United goalscorer at all to people who had seen Rowley, Viollet and Law. O'Farrell was an honest man who saw what was wrong, but in an atmosphere in which players went behind his back to Busby and Edwards, and George Best's genius kept the ship afloat but was increasingly waterlogged with scandal, he was too naive to survive.

It was for an article in which he said that everyone was to blame for United's decline, and not just O'Farrell, that David Meek was banned from travelling with the team, and a unique relationship was lost for ever. The

Evening News was informed by letter. Busby later told David that it had been a board decision.

The week before Christmas 1972, O'Farrell was asked to attend a board meeting at which he, his coach Malcolm Musgrove and the chief scout John Aston senior, left back when United won the Cup in 1948, were sacked. When pressed to give a reason, Louis Edwards replied that it was because of United's League position. Matt Busby did not speak at all. He had already offered the job to Tommy Docherty.

Docherty was the actual creator of the Chelsea team that won the Cup for Dave Sexton in 1970, and had managed Scotland with reasonable success. He allowed his players to express themselves and he was a crude, colourful ruthless personality. In that sense Busby chose well, because it needed a Docherty to put an end to something, and to get rid of the legends Law, Charlton, Crerand and Best, no matter how distastefully some of it was done. And perhaps it needed relegation as well.

In 1973 I was asked to write the opening episodes of a television series set in Australia. I did not want to do it and agreed on condition that they paid for me to go to Sydney, which I never thought they would. I should have known better. The producer was the famously outrageous Tony Essex and he took me with him. On our fourth day there I met Alexandra, who became my second wife, and everything was changed. My life fragmented, and when it reassembled had a different shape. England seemed a long way away, and during the next five years I did not spend much time there.

By chance I made one of my returns on a spring Monday in 1974, on the first Qantas jet ever to land at Manchester, diverted there to refuel by fog. A cleaning crew came aboard and the first of them to walk down the aisle was a lugubrious character of about fifty. I leaned out and said, 'How did they get on?'

'They were relegated,' he said.

When I reached London and newspapers I read that it was Denis Law, given a free transfer by Docherty and snapped up by Manchester City, who had put United down in the last minute of the derby match, with a lightning back-heeled goal that was his last kick in League football. Later that year, on a television set in the garden of a villa on the Tuscan coast, I saw his last game ever, in the World Cup for Scotland against Zaire.

Frustrations

At the end of their regime Matt and Jimmy had concentrated on the first team and Europe without much thought for the future. As their legendary players faded it was clear that the standard of their replacements was much lower, and what the incomers had to do was rebuild. For whatever reason – Matt's hovering presence or the fact that lesser managers sign lesser players – McGuinness, O'Farrell, Docherty, Sexton and Atkinson all failed in one way or another. The Youth Cup victory of 1964 was United's last appearance in the final of that competition until 1992, and between George Best's retirement in 1973 and the arrival of Brian Robson in 1981 there was no truly world-class player at Old Trafford. Near misses by

Dave Sexton and Cup wins for Docherty and Atkinson were fine, but at the same time they were reminders that the gap between the very good and the excellent is huge. If the ballplayers are not the very best, or there is no thoughtful steel to support them, power teams like Don Revie's Leeds will always win. Alex Ferguson knows this, and it is why he won the League at last in 1993. Paradoxically it was the preceding twenty-odd years that more than any others showed the stubborness of the dream, because none of the managers resorted to out-and-out power or the kick and rush. Whatever was happening off the field, they were true to the club's traditions on it: they tried to play beautiful football even when the players fell short. That is why the wait was so frustrating.

My own strongest memories of the 1970s and 80s are to do with spectators. When United were in the Second Division my son and I went to see them at Millwall. Fences had just been erected at Old Trafford, and we decided that since the United crowd was the most violent in the country, and Millwall a volatile venue, we would wear no colours and try to avoid the United support. We finished up standing in the Millwall section, where they were so frustrated by United's victory that a knife fight broke out within a few feet of us. The next time we saw them was at Tottenham, more than a year later. We were with Alexandra and an Australian woman friend, and as we left the ground the crowd panicked at the rumour of a fight down the street. The rush lasted twenty or thirty seconds, but when it stopped the street was half cleared, and littered with shoes that people had shed in their flight. The curious silence of the thing was chilling.

Then when we watched on television the careless 1979

Cup Final loss to Arsenal, an actor who had come to our flat locked himself in the lavatory and fried his brains with cocaine. I took him to the theatre and dumped him at the stage door, although he was in no state to go on. The next time I saw United in a televised Cup Final was in 1983, against Brighton, and I was in a motel in upstate New South Wales. By then of course, the whole sad story of Matt and Big Louis had hit the media.

Profits into loss

The fact is that Louis Edwards loved his work with Manchester United and the League Management Committee to the neglect of his meat business; and his brother Douglas perhaps devoted too much time to the civic career that made him lord mayor and high sheriff of Greater Manchester. In 1973 the business made a profit of £360,000 on a twenty-million-pound turnover, and this was the last year under the Edwards regime that a dividend was declared. That same year Britain joined the Common Market, and EEC rules on quality made trading more difficult. As early as 1966 a report by Manchester City Council had criticised the quality of Edwards's meat, and in 1975 the company lost its Lancashire Education Committee contract and there were redundancies at Miles Platting. There was no improvement in sight and Louis's personal position deteriorated. He sought advice from Professor T. Roland Smith, of Manchester University's

Institute of Science and Technology, a business thinker and expert in the rescue of ailing companies.

Smith's opinion was that Louis should find a buyer for the meat company, and save his personal position through his holding in Manchester United. The way to do this was to declare a rights issue, the sale of new shares to existing shareholders. These shares could be sold on at a profit as well as being used to enormously increase the scope for dividends: in Louis's case from £6,000 to something like £150,000.

Busby was profoundly opposed to the scheme, which was presented as a way to raise money for the club. At the same time he was trapped. Louis's control of United had been the basis of Matt's power, but now Louis wanted to run the thing for himself. The agreements between them were coming to pieces, in particular the deal that each would support the election to the board of the other's son. Martin Edwards was elected in 1970 when he was twenty-five and learning the meat business. He played rugby on Saturdays and was not often at Old Trafford. Sandy Busby was thirty-two in 1970. He had been an unsuccessful professional footballer and worked in bookmaking, which meant that by FA rules he could not be a club director. This objection was circumvented when he went to run the Old Trafford souvenir shop.

When Matt retired in 1969 Louis proposed that he should take a testimonial but Matt refused. He bought a twenty-year lease on the souvenir shop instead, for £10,000 and a nominal rent of £5 a week. This deal was not to be made public. At the same time the board had given Jimmy Murphy a £20,000 settlement, equivalent to five years' salary, and a scouting job at twenty-five pounds a week. They would not pay his home phone bill any more, nor his daily taxi to the ground, and he was made to share an office with Joe Armstrong. Unfortunately, one of the ways in which Wilf McGuinness tried to stand on his own feet was to keep his old mentor at a distance. He did not want Jimmy to scout and Frank O'Farrell did not need him either. Tommy Docherty, for all his faults, had more football sense, and since they were paying Jimmy he brought him back in to do the work. On Jimmy's advice he bought the winger Steve Coppell sight unseen.

Matt's relationship with Jimmy was virtually over, and that with Big Louis had changed. To have any influence at all Matt had to be a party to discussions about the rights issue, and in September 1976 he went with Edwards, Alan Gibson and T. Roland Smith to see the London brokers Kleinwort Benson. As the plan took shape the Edwards family started to buy shares again: in 1977 from the daughters of Walter Crickmer and Harold Hardman, and in 1978 when Martin Edwards took out a £200,000 overdraft to buy 1,100 shares from Alan Gibson, who along with Bill Young agreed to leave the board and become a vice president. In the sense that the buyers had knowledge of the impending rights issue all these were insider deals, which were not at that time illegal.

In the middle of it all Tommy Docherty was sacked. His managership had seen many minor dishonesties and cheap deals behind the scenes, and there had even been notorious ticket touts in the boardroom, but the football had made a fresh start. His team played too much hard stuff at the back, I always thought, and was too frantic, in too much of a hurry and less measured than a true United team, but they had regained the First Division, lost the 1976 Cup Final to Southampton and won it against Liverpool in 1977, when the young United fullback Arthur Albiston had Kevin Keegan in his pocket throughout the game. Docherty, however, had been having a serious three-year affair with the wife of the club physiotherapist Laurie Brown. After winning the Cup he thought that he was safe to make a pre-emptive strike, and sold the story to the *People*.

The idea that a personal and business problem of this sort can be resolved by selling its details to a newspaper instead of having a discussion between the parties might not come first to everyone, and it did not fit the spin-doctored image of United. Nevertheless, Docherty was told not to worry, and it was not until Busby flew back from his holiday in Ireland that the red manure hit the fan. Laurie Brown was called to a board meeting at the Edwards mansion and there have always been rumours that he was about to be given a golden handshake until he threatened to make revelations of his own. Whatever the truth of this there was another meeting at which Docherty was sacked. There was a lot of inspired talk in the papers about United being a club which respected integrity and family values. Soon after, Dave Sexton, honourable in the O'Farrell mould but more worldly, was offered the managership and accepted.

It was an unwholesome episode, and some people have described Matt's intervention as desperate and hypocrit-ical. I am not so sure. I think he knew that Docherty's essential surgery was done and seized on the chance to be rid of him, not caring how it seemed to the world. If there was desperation it was not about Docherty; it was about Matt's need to assert himself and seem indis-pensable, because he must have known, must he not, that his control of the club was slipping away?

Denouement

In August 1978 the board refused to elect Sandy Busby. The meat company lost £340,000 that year, and was prosecuted for bad standards under the Food and Drugs Act. In September the rights issue was put to the board. Les Olive had written a brave letter against it, and Matt argued that the club did not need to raise money in this way: they had 50,000 regular spectators and £450,000 in the Development Association account. The board ignored him and voted in favour. There was controversy in the newspapers and a High Court challenge by the wealthy supporter John Fletcher, owner of Trumanns Steel. But it was to no avail, and in December the rights issue was approved by an extraordinary general meeting. Four days later Edwards passed control of the near-bankrupt meat company to the entrepreneur James Gulliver for something like £100,000 plus shares. Gulliver renamed it the Argyll Group, which ten years later was worth £1.7 billion. The Edwards family were to sell their share for eight million pounds.

Martin Edwards took out a further overdraft of £400,000 to pay for his share of the rights issue. James Gulliver bought some 100,000 of Louis Edwards's shares for £250,000 and went on the United board. Matt abstained from the vote: he said that he did not know who James

Gulliver was. The club made a mere one million pounds from the rights issue. Dave Sexton spent £700,000 on Ray Wilkins, his Chelsea midfielder, and was told to sell other players to make up the money.

It was all legal, but nobody liked it, and it was Matt's opposition that alerted investigative journalists.

On 28 January 1980 Granada TV's *World in Action* series screened an edition entitled 'The Man Who Bought United'. It explained how Big Louis had used Frank Farrington to buy shares in the 1960s, and the purpose of the rights issue, and how United had a slush fund to acquire youth players. Most damagingly, it revealed that the Edwards meat business had been built up by the systematic bribery and corruption of public officials, and how action by local authorities to clean up their purchasing systems had led to the loss of the lucrative contracts. One of the people from various levels of life who received regular free meat parcels was shown to be Alan Hardaker, the holier-than-thou secretary of the Football League, the man who vilified George Best for retaliation against being kicked black and blue, who believed that English football had nothing to learn from Europe and sought to keep United out of it.

Martin Edwards has called the Granada programme 'a complete character assassination', and it did of course present events as a cunning plot from day one, which it never had been. It had if anything been a folly of love and ambition; but Louis, who more than most people had wanted to be merry and liked, was shown to be shady at the very least. He went to pieces, and a month after the programme was screened died from a heart attack while taking a bath.

When I read it in the papers I could not but think of Jack Wood and champagne in Munich.

Martin Edwards, the watchful teenager who had never perhaps been very interested in soccer, now owned its most mythical club. He soon flexed his muscles. He fired the decent but plodding Sexton, hired the ebullient Ron Atkinson and voted Bobby Charlton onto the board, a decision of real wisdom. In time he felt himself strong enough to take the souvenir shop away from the ageing Busby. He then sacked Atkinson, engaged Ferguson, and was a prime mover in the conspiracy to form the Premier League. He turned the club itself into a PLC and his own holding into an enormous fortune. But the fans never warmed to him, and for Martin himself the dream seems to have been a heavy burden.

His attempts to sell the club to Robert Maxwell, to Michael Knighton and to BSkyB, and his release of huge tranches of his own shares were, I believe, as much attempts to get out from under as to make money. Finally he did get out and, whatever else he has done, I was glad for him. He and his mother are the most enigmatic figures in United's story, and the damage that it did to them is private.

Same old game, Arthur

I don't remember the last time I saw Jimmy Murphy, but he never did leave my head from the first day I met him, and I have been told that I was in his. Busby I last saw in January 1983. We had been living in France and were about to go to Australia for what turned out to be almost five years. My son got tickets for a game against Nottingham Forest, and he, Alexandra and I sat high up at the Stretford End to watch Ron Atkinson's United, which was almost the real thing but not quite. Busby came out onto the pitch to receive some award. He was club president, having retired from the board because he could not influence it, although he still went to Old Trafford every day. Lady Jean was lost to Alzheimer's and Matt himself had survived a minor stroke. He was seventy-four years old, wore his trademark brown suit and raised his arm in an imperial salute.

'My God,' said Alexandra, 'even from here you can see that he's a shit.' Then she acknowledged the charisma, the extraordinary force of the man, as it filled the wintry arena.

Her glimpse of the dreamer is the end of my story, really, except that one evening in Sydney the phone rang and it was Arthur Walmsley to say that Jack Smith was dead. Then when I was back in England he told me that

Jimmy was ill but that they had spoken on the phone. Only then did Arthur learn how Busby and the board had stopped Jimmy's taxi and other little perks. With six children, Jimmy had a rich private world but was not well off. The man who was so fierce in the cause was too proud to fight for himself. After they stopped the taxi he went to Old Trafford on the train but never paid. The ticket collectors knew who he was and waved him through.

During one call Arthur asked Jimmy what he thought about modern football.

'Same old game, Arthur,' came the hoarse reply. 'Easy when you've got the ball. Bloody hard when you've not.'

Then one day in 1989 I read that he was dead. It is said that towards the end he was sad and would go to the pub in old clothes. Matt never visited him in hospital.

Later I heard two stories about Jimmy. One was from Arnie Sidebottom, the Yorkshire and England seam bowler, at Willis Hall's sixty-fifth birthday in Bradford. Sidebottom had a brief career at United in the early 1970s, when as he said, 'I was all long hair and in the gear. This old man stared at me for a couple of days and then he gave me a fiver and said, "Arnie, for Christ's sake get your hair cut."'

The other story I heard from one of Jimmy's sons at the bust unveiling. Ron Atkinson asked Jimmy for some advice because he could not make up his mind about the centre forward Gary Birtles.

'You can't?' exclaimed Jimmy. 'I made up mine after five minutes.'

The same son, in a splendid malapropism, said that all of them at home had been amazed, during Jimmy's last years, by some of the clichés he came out with.

Matt was a great and extraordinary man, I realise, but

Jimmy Murphy was my hero, and although I am old now he still is and always will be, because I would like to have done in my work what he did in his. He was a hard man for excellence but vulnerable in life, who wanted credit for what he had done but would not take it for what he had not; a cynical innocent who was passionate, and chuckled, and liked whisky and sugar and hot water, and who came out with the clichés. 'When you put on a red shirt,' goes the best of them, delivered in many a harangue, 'you're the greatest player in the world, even when you know you're not.'

Bonus Material and Extras

Nowadays no self-respecting DVD comes without its Bonus Material and Extras, so why shouldn't a book? Writer's Commentary. The Real Historical Background. Deleted Scenes, or in this case, Deleted Sidelights, such as: What would happen if teams of the 1950s could be brought back to play floodlit friendlies against today's champions? The answer is that before they could do so they would have to recognise that the single biggest change in the way football is played is due to improved sports medicine, diet and fitness regimes, so that players recover more effectively from their injuries and can sustain a high tempo for much longer. Teams from the 50s would have to undergo this conditioning process, but having done so they would to some degree be liberated, because their boots and shin pads and old leather footballs were so cumbersome, and they played much of the time on muddy or bone-hard pitches that we would consider unfit. Due to the influx of money and foreigners the average standard of football in England is higher, but the best players would be good in any epoch, and there were more highly skilled English-born players in 1950 than there are today. This is the paradox, as I have tried to show, of half a century of people who learned to play in the streets and at a minor competitive level, followed by half a century of mainly misdirected coaching.

I have an actor friend named John Salthouse, who under his real name John Lewis captained the England youth team in the era of Alan Hudson but snapped his Achilles tendon as soon as he turned pro and had to give up. A while ago he complained to me about how little football coaching allowed youngsters to develop early skills in a non-pressured environment and I said, 'How long have you been an actor?'

'Thirty years.'

'How many directors made a serious difference?'

John has been in big movies, television series, the West End and the National Theatre, and after a moment he said, 'Four.' One of whom had died some years previously.

So there is always the issue stressed by Matt Busby: top talent, and how little of it there is to go round. But there are helpful environments, and United under Ferguson is one of them. I saw him play once, in a pre-season friendly at Highbury. Drunken Rangers fans pissed into bottles and threw them. Arsenal won with ease, although to the end Ferguson threw himself at their defence in a sort of half-skilful, bloody-minded fury. He was raw and bedraggled on the day but there was a sense of space around him, like there is around a wonderful actor. At the time this was unsettling because there did not seem to be an explanation.

There was one, of course, but it came later, in the cruise to so many victories, the endless drive to be on top, the hairdryer in Gary Pallister's face and the boot in David Beckham's; and at Old Trafford in the creation of three great teams, the latest one being almost as brilliant going forward as the Law, Best and Charlton outfit, and far better in defence.

Ferguson is the most successful manager in British football history, and who is to say that he has not been the best? He has not changed the idea of the game, perhaps, in the way that Chapman did, nor, as Matt did, become a legend beyond football. Yet after all, if we live long enough we learn that all young men lose their powers, that rivals are insistent, that tomorrow will always bring defeat, and that dreams of any kind do not often come true, and that when they do their taste has left us by the morning.

In the realms of memory and dreams it is easy for one to become the other, so that neither have truth or value, and yet at the same time our memories are our dreams, because they are of things that we wish to change or make happen again. For those worn old men who had seen Meredith and Charlie Roberts and stood at the Stretford End when I was a youth, Matt and Jimmy did make dreams come true, and so has Ferguson for the likes of me, who saw Carey and Rowley and Duncan Edwards and Tommy Taylor, the leader of the line.

Manchester was the place in history where men and women discovered that their lives and humanity were worth less than the machines they tended, and it is from their profound objection to this that the city has derived its capacity to renew itself. The hand-loom weavers who in 1819 marched to Peterloo knew that a few years before there had been salmon in the stinking factory-polluted River Irwell, just as the youths from heartless tower blocks who became the musicians of Tony Wilson's Madchester knew that Margaret Thatcher did not have the final say on who was of use to the world and who was not. And from the stench of the chemical works at the Newton Heath ground to the Theatre of Dreams and Mid-Eastlands, both halves of the city, red and blue, asserted their idealism in their demand for beautiful football.

I am too young to have seen Matt or Peter Doherty play for Manchester City, although I wish I had, but I am not too old to look forward to the unrealised dream: the domination of Europe with football as graceful as that of di Stéfano and Kopa and Hector Rial, and the victory in Latin America. But as Matt once said to me, 'You'd have to have a very good team to go there.'

What a friend we have in Jesus
He is watching from above
And He sent to us a saviour
His name is Eric Cantona!

Oooh-ah the Cantona!

Actually, Eric Cantona is the only other player I saw who had the same natural all-over-the-field game as di Stéfano, and he has a link with a particular childhood memory.

On the night of the Manchester Blitz my father was on Home Guard duty, and put out gas-main fires caused by a bomber that dumped its load too early. Next day he drove into the city, and when he returned described how, on Deansgate, Forsyth's music shop had been blown apart, and pianos lay smashed on the roadway. Fifty years later, rebuilt, it was where Eric Cantona bought his trumpet. Cantona was the most eccentric of all United's heroes, and Jimmy Murphy would have relished him. In fact, I can see Jim's eyes glitter and feel him nudge me as Joe Armstrong launches into the chaff.

'Hey up, Eric. Heard the one about the trawler and the seagulls?'

All right, my old pal? All right, Jim. I wrote this for you, in the hope that other people will get the message, like Matt did at Bari.

Bibliography

Almanaco Illustrato del Calcio, Pancini, published annually

Busby, Matt, *My Story*, Souvenir Press, 1957

Clarke, Alf, *Manchester United*, Convoy Books, 1951

Crick, Michael, *The Man Who Bought United*, Granada TV, 1980

Dunphy, Eamon, *A Strange Kind of Glory*, Heinemann, 1991

Glanvill, Rick, *Sir Matt Busby*, Virgin/Manchester United Books, 1994

Glanville, Brian, *Soccer Nemesis*, Secker & Warburg, 1955

Green, Geoffrey, *The History of the Football Association*, Naldrett, 1953

Hints on Association Football, John Player & Sons cigarette cards, pre-1939

Knight, Ken, Kobylecki, John and Van Hoof, Serge, *A History of the World Cup. Volume 1: The Jules Rimet Years*, Heart Books, 1998

Mason, Tony, *Association Football and English Society*, Harvester, 1980

Official Illustrated Manchester United Encyclopaedia, Manchester United Books, 1998

Roberts, John, *The Team That Wouldn't Die*, Arthur Barker, 1975

Rollin, Jack, *Rothman's Book of Football Records*, Headline, 1998

Taylor, Frank, *The Day a Team Died*, Stanley Paul, 1960

Acknowledgements

There are always people who stand in the shadow of a book, but have contributed to what can seem to be the impact of the author alone. In this case I must cast light and gratitude upon Eve Pearce and Alan Dewhurst for having saved and dug out photos and memorabilia; Emma Dewhurst and Richard Linford for their word-processing; Gordon Wise at Curtis Brown for selling the book with such acumen and enthusiasm; Tristan Jones et al. at Yellow Jersey for splendid editing and back-up; Alan Plater for noting an error of fact; John Salthouse for the football conversations and his mate Daz in Manchester for the tickets; David Meek for helping out; my wife and play agent Alexandra Cann for her belief and unfailing good judgement; and Capa, who is a dog, and gets along very well with his illiteracy and total ignorance of football. But then, he has God's gift of living in the moment.

Keith Dewhurst, London, 2009

List of Illustrations

List of Illustrations

Index

275

Index

Index

Index

Index

Index

Index

Index